# Amy-Jill Levine

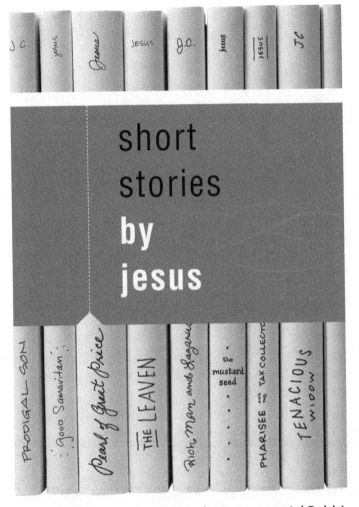

short
stories
**by**
jesus

The Enigmatic Parables of a Controversial Rabbi

Participant Guide
by Maria Mayo

Abingdon Press / Nashville

SHORT STORIES BY JESUS
The Enigmatic Parables of a Controversial Rabbi
Participant Guide

978-1-5018-5816-1

18 19 20 21 22 23 24 25 26 27 — 10 9 8 7 6 5 4 3 2 1
MANUFACTURED IN THE UNITED STATES OF AMERICA

# Contents

Apr 3 Mar. 27

Apr. 3

April 10

# Contents

# Introduction

In *Short Stories by Jesus: The Enigmatic Parables of a Controversial Rabbi*, Amy-Jill Levine uses her scholarship on first-century Jewish history to hear Jesus as a Jewish teacher speaking to a Jewish audience. Her point is not to dismiss any helpful Christian interpretations that have been made of the parables over the past two thousand years. Rather, she seeks to recover their original provocation and so help to explain why people first decided to follow Jesus. In her work on the parables, she tries to imagine what these short stories would have sounded like to people who had no idea that one day Jesus would be recognized as divine, or even that he would be crucified. How would these people have heard the words of this Jewish storyteller? And how can those same stories, two thousand years later, challenge us to look deep into our own lives?

Parables are stories that are sometimes only one or two sentences long. Much of Jesus's teaching was introduced in parables, and the Gospel writers left most of the parables without interpretation so we can figure them out ourselves.

Every reader will hear something different, and the parables may mean different things over time. Audiences get different interpretations from the parables depending on where they are, what their experiences have been, or what challenges they're facing in their lives. For example, the story of the Pearl of Great Price might mean more to a woman who owns and appreciates many fine jewels than it would to someone who lacks access to such luxury items. Or it might mean less. Certainly, their understanding of the story, of the merchant who sells all he has to buy a single pearl, and of an expensive and breathtaking piece of jewelry, will be different. Instead of reducing each parable to a single meaning, we do well to leave all avenues open for different interpretations.

Even as we delve into how the original audience might have heard the parables, we should also be aware of how they affect us in the present day. "What makes the parables mysterious, or difficult," Levine writes, "is that they challenge us to look into the hidden aspects of our own values, our own lives." It can be uncomfortable to leave a text open to multiple interpretations, but this may be the challenge inherent in the parables.

Jesus is not a "one size fits all" teacher: some people he called to abandon everything; others he asked to provide hospitality. For still others, he simply granted a healing or forgiveness; others he asked to remember his teachings. Paul, too, tells us that different people have different callings and different gifts. Therefore, we should expect to see different things in the parables.

Levine points out that "religion has been defined as designed to comfort the afflicted and to afflict the comfortable." We know from the parables in the Old Testament that parables serve to do the afflicting. That is, they challenge us to look deep into our hearts, to learn something about ourselves that we may have ignored, to learn more about our faith and our values. If we find that we really like a parable because we've got it all figured out so it doesn't continue to challenge us, we are probably not reading very well.

The key to a parable, as we will see in this volume, is to figure out what part of it challenges you and makes you uncomfortable. Does the parable "afflict" you? Then you are probably on the right track.

We should also resist the urge to turn the parables into allegories or platitudes. When we settle for easy interpretations—be nice like the good Samaritan; we will be forgiven like the prodigal son; we should pray like the widow—we miss the point of parables. Levine advises readers: "We might be better off thinking less about what they 'mean' and more about what they can 'do': remind, provoke, refine, confront, disturb...."

Part of understanding the parables and recognizing their challenge is to dig into the history that surrounds them. Context matters, and context reveals a lot about how and what these parables mean. If we consider the original audience, and the original place and time these stories were told, we hear details and challenges that we might not hear now if we only read them in the comfort of our homes and Christian context. We know who Jesus is, and we might tend to hear his words based on that. But at the time he was telling these stories, there was no Christian context. Jesus was just a Jewish storyteller, one of many, and so how might his stories have resonated with and provoked listeners in the specific times and places they were told?

One of the values of Levine's text comes in digging into this history and identifying the original context of these parables. Doing so helps today's reader separate what is normal from what is absurd. It's important to know how Jews and Samaritans regarded each other, and how day laborers and vineyard owners figured out their working relationships. It is important to know what options were open to women in antiquity in terms of family life and finances; it is important to know how fathers and sons were expected to relate to each other. If we don't know anything about

Pharisees or tax collectors, or who went into the Temple, we don't know whether what we are hearing in the parables is something that happens every day or something far out of the ordinary. When parables are read without regard to their historical context, the door is open for incorrect or problematic readings.

Levine provides a keen analogy for how important context can be to understanding a story. She reminisces about the children's television cartoon *The Rocky and Bullwinkle Show* and its cast of mysteriously named characters. Children would have seen a moose and a squirrel up to all kinds of shenanigans, endless entertainment for the under-ten set. What children missed, though, was the social satire embedded in the program. Children didn't know why the bad guys had Russian names like Boris Badenov and Natasha Fatale. They wouldn't have associated Boris with Boris Godunov, the czar, let alone the play by Alexander Pushkin or the opera by Modest Mussorgsky; they would not have understood that Natasha was a "femme fatale." As a young child, Levine could appreciate the moose and the squirrel, but not the sharp social commentary that the cartoon also offered. She lacked the context.

Parables are like this. We can understand them as children's stories and find them amusing or offering a simple moral point. But if we hear them as adults, and if we hear them in their original contexts, they are even more profound. Their deeper meaning depends on an understanding of what's going on in the world around the stories.

The context for Jesus's stories includes not only the historical world of first-century Judea and Galilee within the broader Roman Empire, but also Israel's sacred scriptures and the echoes they would evoke among Jesus's Jewish hearers. The parable of the Prodigal Son begins, "There was a man who had two sons," and this would immediately remind readers of other men with two sons: Adam's Cain and Abel, Abraham's Ishmael and Isaac, Isaac's Jacob and Esau. Understanding this literary context sheds light on the meanings and expectations in the parable. Similarly, knowing the historical reality behind the parable helps illuminate the subtle interactions and messages it contains. For example, Jesus's original listeners would have been well aware of the enmity between Jews and Samaritans, and this would have made the actions in the parable of the Good Samaritan seem even more outrageous. They would know that tax collectors collaborate with the Roman Empire; they would have seen Pharisees as generally righteous individuals.

We learn from Levine's chapters on the parables that our best strategy is to read them as the first audiences did, and to try to recover the original challenge. This is difficult, because we don't know for sure if Jesus actually told the parables that appear in the Gospels, although Levine is fairly confident that he did. We also don't know who was listening or how they reacted, because it is doubtful that Jesus told the stories only once or exactly the same way every time. Each time he told them, new audiences may well have come away with new interpretations.

It is likely that Jesus actually did tell the parables presented in the Gospels for these reasons:

- They reflect themes that are concerns of Jesus elsewhere, such as economics (what happens to the poor, mutual dependence), relationships (families, neighbors, mutual reciprocity, humility), and prioritizing (choose life, determine what is necessary, practicality should give way to generosity, the kingdom is coming with or without our help).

- The parables match Jesus's comments about himself and the kingdom.
- The parables frequently use the motif of celebration. Jesus likes to celebrate, and throughout the Gospels we see him at the table with various guests or in the crowd feeding everyone. The parables reflect this, such as the celebration at the end of the parable of the Prodigal Son.
- The fact that the evangelists try so hard to interpret and control the parables is another reason to think that Jesus actually did tell these stories. We see Luke trying to "domesticate," or tame, the parable of the Widow and the Judge by telling the reader before it begins that the story is actually about prayer. Yet the parable is not about a widow who closes her door and then gets on her knees to pray; it is about a widow who appears in the public court and threatens a judge with a black eye. Were the story an invention of the evangelist, there would be no need to explain or alter its purpose.

Another interpretive trap we should be careful not to fall into is the tendency to read the parables as allegories. Allegorical readings assign a symbolic role to every element in the parable—the man who lost his sheep stands for God, the lost sheep is a repentant sinner—but such readings don't always make sense in the original context or the actual wording of the parable. In the parable of the Lost Sheep, there is *no mention of a shepherd*, and the sheep owner himself *lost* the sheep. Therefore, to jump immediately to identifying this sheep owner with God is not necessary. Similarly, interpreting the Good Samaritan as Jesus, who comes to save us from death as the Samaritan rescues the man by the side of the road, is not a necessary understanding of the parable. Much more is going on. The parables have to make sense without any knowledge of the rest of Jesus's story. As Levine writes, "Sometimes a shepherd is just a shepherd, and…a king may be just a king." The stories pack a punch in other ways without the symbolic overload.

However, even though historical context is essential, the meaning of parables should not be limited just to this. These stories must speak to us across the centuries and continue to live; otherwise they stop being scripture or literature. The primary questions are these: "How do we hear the parables through an imagined set of first-century Jewish ears [Levine helps us here], and then how do we translate them so that they can be heard still speaking?"

As we listen for the parables to bring meaning to the present day, we must also be careful that we don't infect Jesus's stories with anti-Judaism. Sometimes we bring incorrect stereotypes about early Judaism to the parables, and when we do, our interpretations get off track. For example, if we think of the God of the Old Testament as angry or wrathful and then see Jesus proclaiming a different God, we are not reading correctly. The God of Jesus *is* the God of the Old Testament.

---

**We should also be careful not to let the parables become only simple platitudes. Parables are more than just moral statements: they are designed to challenge, to entertain, and to encourage our imaginations.**

---

We should also be careful not to let the parables become only simple platitudes. Parables are more than just moral statements: they are designed to challenge, to entertain, and to encourage our imaginations.

Where reading the Bible is concerned, we often don't listen as well as we could. Sometimes we miss what is provocative about the parable, sometimes we just apply simplistic interpretations, and other times we bring in negative interpretations that Jesus would never have meant or even tolerated. Levine calls this "auditory atrophy," and she gives these reasons for why it occurs as we misread the parables:

- In some churches, parables are only children's stories. This leads to overly simplistic interpretations. If we remain with the interpretations we learned as children, we fail to take Jesus seriously as a teacher of adults.
- Many clergy don't work to understand what is provocative in the parable. This often happens because church services are designed more for comfort than for challenge.
- Congregations see the sermon as entertainment. "When church becomes a club, parables become pedestrian."
- Clergy make use of anti-Jewish stereotypes, such as by comparing "bad" Judaism to "good" Jesus or making the parable of the Mustard Seed about purity laws.
- Homiletics (the study of giving sermons) no longer focuses on history and the biblical text as much as on communications theory or in telling a good story. "The more time we take in finding our own context and so our own voice, the less attention gets paid to Jesus's own context and voice." We can think of three contexts for

the parables: what is going on at the time Jesus told them (the world behind the text), what is going on in the rest of the Gospel where we find the parable (the world in the text), and how we understand the parable in our own lives (the world in front of the text). All three settings are important if we are more fully to understand these wonderful short stories.

In her volume, Levine offers her take on the parables of Jesus. Her chapters are "works of history and imagination, of critical analysis and playful speculation." She finds the parables provocative, inspirational, beautiful, and meaningful. And yet Levine is a Jewish scholar who hears Jesus as she would hear an ancient rabbi. As she insists, "One need not have to believe in Jesus as Lord and Savior in order to realize that he had some extraordinary things to say."

Each chapter in Levine's volume opens with her "fairly literal" translation of one of the parables. Her translations are challenges in themselves; they make the parable seem unfamiliar, and the reader is forced to listen with new ears. These translations make us pay attention to the words used in the parable, and they force us to slow down when we read. That way, we can hear the parable anew. She then puts each parable in its historical and literary context and corrects interpretations that import negative readings and distort Jesus's message. She finishes by giving fresh readings of what the parables might have meant to those earliest listeners and how we might use the parables' messages today.

In this Participant Guide, you'll find summaries of six chapters of Amy-Jill Levine's *Short Stories by Jesus: The Enigmatic Parables of a Controversial Rabbi.* Each session in the Participant Guide is organized into four sections:

- "The Parable" begins the session with a rendering of the passage from the New Revised Standard Version of the Bible.
- "Chapter Summary" explains the main concepts and themes lifted up in Levine's corresponding chapter.
- "Questions for Reflection" inspire deeper thought and connection to the chapter's main concepts and themes.
- "Personal Response" offers book excerpts with journal prompts for your contemplation.

This book functions as a tour guide for *Short Stories by Jesus*, providing explanations and prompting reflection about Levine's work. Let this study serve as a welcoming table around which we can join in conversation about Jesus's parables and the messages and challenges they delivered to their earliest audiences and bring anew to readers in today's world.

## Session 1

# Lost Sheep, Lost Coin, Lost Son

### THE PARABLES

*So he told them this parable: "Which one of you, having a hundred sheep and losing one of them, does not leave the ninety-nine in the wilderness and go after the one that is lost until he finds it? When he has found it, he lays it on his shoulders and rejoices. And when he comes home, he calls together his friends and neighbors, saying to them, 'Rejoice with me, for I have found my sheep that was lost.' Just so, I tell you, there will be more joy in heaven over one sinner who repents than over ninety-nine righteous persons who need no repentance."*

*Luke 15:3-7*

*"Or what woman having ten silver coins, if she loses one of them, does not light a lamp, sweep the house, and search carefully until she finds it? When*

she has found it, she calls together her friends and neighbors, saying, 'Rejoice with me, for I have found the coin that I had lost.' Just so, I tell you, there is joy in the presence of the angels of God over one sinner who repents."

*Luke 15:8-10*

Then Jesus said, "There was a man who had two sons. The younger of them said to his father, 'Father, give me the share of the property that will belong to me.' So he divided his property between them. A few days later the younger son gathered all he had and traveled to a distant country, and there he squandered his property in dissolute living. When he had spent everything, a severe famine took place throughout that country, and he began to be in need. So he went and hired himself out to one of the citizens of that country, who sent him to his fields to feed the pigs. He would gladly have filled himself with the pods that the pigs were eating; and no one gave him anything. But when he came to himself he said, 'How many of my father's hired hands have bread enough and to spare, but here I am dying of hunger! I will get up and go to my father, and I will say to him, "Father, I have sinned against heaven and before you; I am no longer worthy to be called your son; treat me like one of your hired hands."' So he set off and went to his father. But while he was still far off, his father saw him and was filled with compassion; he ran and put his arms around him and kissed him. Then the son said to him, 'Father, I have sinned against heaven and before you; I am no longer worthy to be called your son.' But the father

16

said to his slaves, 'Quickly, bring out a robe—the best one—and put it on him; put a ring on his finger and sandals on his feet. And get the fatted calf and kill it, and let us eat and celebrate; for this son of mine was dead and is alive again; he was lost and is found!' And they began to celebrate.

"Now his elder son was in the field; and when he came and approached the house, he heard music and dancing. He called one of the slaves and asked what was going on. He replied, 'Your brother has come, and your father has killed the fatted calf, because he has got him back safe and sound.' Then he became angry and refused to go in. His father came out and began to plead with him. But he answered his father, 'Listen! For all these years I have been working like a slave for you, and I have never disobeyed your command; yet you have never given me even a young goat so that I might celebrate with my friends. But when this son of yours came back, who has devoured your property with prostitutes, you killed the fatted calf for him!' Then the father said to him, 'Son, you are always with me, and all that is mine is yours. But we had to celebrate and rejoice, because this brother of yours was dead and has come to life; he was lost and has been found.'"

*Luke 15:11-32*

## CHAPTER SUMMARY

As told in the Gospel of Luke, these three parables (most often called the parable of the Lost Sheep, the parable of the Lost Coin, and the parable of the Prodigal Son) are about human repentance and God's forgiveness. However, this interpretation turns the parables into allegories, and this clearly isn't how a first-century audience would have heard them. The Prodigal Son might have repentance on his mind, but it's hard to imagine a sheep or coin with the ability to repent. In Amy-Jill Levine's estimation, the younger brother in the third parable isn't motivated by repentance, either.

Parables should not need outside answer keys to help us interpret them. In a first-century context, the stories have to have some meaning that the people could understand. More, if Jesus wanted to talk about repenting, he could easily do so without using a parable. As he states, quite directly, "Repent, and believe in the good news" (Mark 1:15).

What if we reconsidered the titles of the first two parables? "The Shepherd Who Lost His Sheep" and "The Woman Who Lost Her Coin" move the emphasis to the one doing the losing, and might capture something closer to what the parables originally meant. Here we already know that, at least on a first reading, neither the sheep owner nor the woman represents God, because God does not lose us.

Next, moving that same emphasis to the last parable yields, "The Father Who Lost His Son(s)." Might the father have been partly responsible for what happened? We tend to focus on the Prodigal, but since the parable begins, "There was a man who had two sons," we should also pay attention both to the father and to the older brother.

Across history, these parables have had various titles revealing various interests among interpreters. Among these have been "The Prodigal and the Prudent" (St. Jerome [347–420]), "The Clever Son" (Lebanese Christians), and Levine's own contribution (on more cynical days), "The Absent Mother." Titles matter.

As we read in the Introduction, parables are not allegories. Remember that allegories are texts that require decoder rings to understand, where each element symbolically represents something else. An allegory would be the beloved Narnia books by C. S. Lewis; those who have the answer key know that Aslan the lion represents Jesus. Another famous allegory is George Orwell's *Animal Farm*, which on the surface is a book about farm animals, pigs and horses and sheep, but which, for those who have the answer key, is really a cautionary tale about Russian communism.

Closer to Jesus's own time period are the allegories known as "Aesop's Fables." For example, Aesop's story of the Tortoise and the Hare has both a surface meaning and a deeper meaning. This story is about a hare and a tortoise engaging in a footrace: surprisingly, the slower tortoise unexpectedly beats the usually fast rabbit. In this story, the hare represents people who have natural talents, such as being able to run fast, but either waste them or rely only on what comes naturally to them rather than on working hard. The tortoise represents those who work hard and diligently, and who succeed even if they were not born with certain talents or abilities. The race represents life itself. Thus, the story tells us that we must work hard and persevere, like the tortoise, and we should not rely only on the talents that come naturally to us. In this story, the decoder ring would reveal, the tortoise equals hard-working people, the hare equals lazy individuals, and the race equals life.

But Jesus's teachings are not simplistic allegories like Aesop's fables or *Animal Farm*. Nor are they extremely complex allegories like the Narnia tales. They are short stories designed less to teach us something new than to remind us of those Kingdom values that we have buried deep down, that we'd rather not let up to the surface. Jesus tells us that "the gate is narrow and the road is hard that leads to life…" (Matthew 7:14). The parables help us go through the gate and stay on the path by challenging us.

## Sometimes a story is just a story. And that story can be amazingly profound and challenging.

An allegorical interpretation of the parable of the Lost Sheep might cast the sheep as a believer who wandered away from the flock and the shepherd as Jesus doing everything to bring the lost sheep back to safety. The ones who are celebrating at the end represent the rejoicing church. This is certainly a good message, but it lacks the challenge that Levine sees in parables. It also requires us to turn the man who has a hundred sheep (that is, a fairly wealthy man) into a shepherd. Jesus can certainly use the term "shepherd" when he wants to, so we should pay attention to the words he does use. Likewise, readings of the parable of the Lost Son that turn the father into God, the prodigal into a repenting Christian, and the brother out in the fields into a Jew (or, even worse, a "Pharisee," which is never a compliment) bring on anti-Jewish readings, mask the challenge, and disregard how Jesus's own audience would have heard the parable in their context. Parables, like these three, are best interpreted not as allegories but as straightforward stories meant to challenge or provoke. Sometimes a story is just a story. And that story can be amazingly profound and challenging.

### The Parable of the Lost Sheep

Most traditional interpretations hold that the lost sheep is a believer who has wandered away from the flock, the one searching is Jesus or a representative of Jesus, and the friends who feast at the end are the church. Such allegorical readings miss the challenge of the parable. They are not "wrong" per se, but they do not appreciate fully the genius of Jesus's teaching.

We are first introduced to the idea of the parable as an allegory by Luke, the evangelist who relates this story. He writes, "Just so, I tell you, there will be more joy in heaven over one sinner who repents than over ninety-nine righteous persons who need no repentance" (15:7). Here, the lost sheep represents "one sinner who repents," and the flock stands in for "ninety-nine righteous." However, the parable suggests no behavior difference among the lost sheep and the ninety-nine remaining in the flock. The allegory doesn't match the parable. There was no sin. There was no repentance. And anyway, how can a sheep either sin or repent? The sheep were presumably just standing there, bleating. Except for the lost-then-found one, who might have been annoyed to find himself hoisted on the man's shoulders. Sheep can be very large, and carrying a sheep on one's shoulders wouldn't have been easy— or comfortable—for either the sheep owner or the sheep! If Jesus wanted to talk about how God loves us and forgives us, he could do so directly. Moreover, that was not a point he needed to make to his Jewish audience, because that audience already knew that God loves us and forgives us. Something else must be going on with the sheep owner who lost his sheep.

Later interpreters also read the parable as an allegory. Still others bring anti-Jewish stereotypes to the text, assuming that Jewish audiences would have disliked laborers and refused to do the job of a shepherd. Thus, they assume that the parable recovers a positive role for shepherds and challenges social conventions. However, there is no reason to believe that Jews of the time would have had anything negative to say about shepherds, and Levine shows how Jewish texts bear this out. Nor, again, does the parable ever mention shepherds. The parable doesn't present negative images of Jews in order to make Jesus look good. The parable is not, at least without Luke's allegorizing, a story about repentance and forgiving. The sheep did not sin or repent; the sheep owner is actually at fault for losing the sheep. Finally, that party at the end is strange: Why would the sheep owner want to celebrate the finding of one sheep? Why in fact would the friends and neighbors care? Rather, Levine concludes, the parable is challenging in an altogether different way.

The shepherd realizes he has lost one of his flock. He sees that one sheep is missing out of the hundred sheep he owns. But how does he know this? He cannot ask the sheep to line up in groups of ten. The sheep are not wearing sweatshirts with numbers. The only way he knows his sheep is missing is because he has counted them. Once he realizes his flock is incomplete, he sets out to search. When he finds the sheep, he has an exaggerated celebration by himself, and then he invites his friends and neighbors to celebrate with him. What joy can we experience when we find what we have lost? And, this sheep owner knows when one of a hundred sheep is missing. Do we know what—or whom—we have lost? Do we count what—or who—is present? Do we take responsibility for losing something, or someone? And will we make an effort to find what, or whom, we've lost?

## The Parable of the Lost Coin

Some commentators assume that the challenging message in this parable is the presence of a woman as a main character. They assume the context is a rigid Jewish social system in which women have no freedom, authority, or agency. However, anyone who thinks of early Judaism this way must have missed reading much of the Old Testament[1]—Esther and Ruth, for two examples, are women who play significant roles. Some Christian Bibles also have the book of Judith, and she is quite a heroine. Just as a sheep owner would not have been an offensive or unattractive main character, a woman would have been equally unremarkable. In fact, the parable, like the other stories of women in the Gospels, shows us that Jewish women of the time had access to their own funds, could have their own celebrations, and owned their own homes! Luke even tells us that they served as patrons for Jesus and his other followers by providing them financial support (see Luke 8:1-3). And, just as with the parable of the Lost Sheep, this parable does not need to create a negative vision of Judaism in order to surprise and provoke listeners. Something else is going on.

The woman in this parable discovers that her collection of ten coins is incomplete and that she is missing one. She is likely a woman of some means, considering that she has a set of ten drachmas at all. A drachma was worth about the same as a denarius, one day's wage for a laborer,[2] and two of these were enough to pay for a stay at the inn for the Good Samaritan earlier in Luke's Gospel (10:35). Like the shepherd who noticed one missing from one hundred, the woman counts and realizes that one coin is missing. Like the shepherd, again, she launches an exaggerated search. Unlike the shepherd, however, when the woman finds the coin, she celebrates "the coin that I had lost" (15:9); that is, she explicitly takes responsibility for losing the coin. Her comment provokes the listener. We celebrate finding what we lose, but do we take responsibility for losing?

---

1   In this Participant Guide, we will refer to the Hebrew Scriptures and the Old Testament interchangeably.

2   James A. Metzger, "Drachma" in *The New Interpreter's Dictionary of the Bible Volume 2*, gen. ed. Katharine D. Sakenfeld (Nashville, TN: Abingdon Press, 2007), 161.

She then throws a party. The Greek words let us know that she invited other women: the nouns are in the feminine. Thus, we realize from this parable that it was perfectly normal for women to entertain their friends.

As before, Luke comes in at the end and provides an interpretation. He writes, "'Just so, I tell you, there is joy in the presence of the angels of God over one sinner who repents'" (15:10). Even though neither the sheep nor the coin did anything of note, Luke assumes that they represent sinners who demonstrate a change of heart. As Levine points out, there is no such thing as either sheep shame or penny penitence. The coin and the sheep did not sin, and they did not repent. Nor do the sheep owner or the woman "forgive" their lost objects. Something else must be going on.

And for readers who take the allegorical route and conclude that the sheep owner in the first parable and the father in the third parable represent God, why not this woman with the coins as well? Levine would like this woman to be an image of God as well, but in her reading, she sees the sheep owner as a man with one hundred sheep, the woman as a woman with ten coins, and the father as a man with two sons. The challenge of all three parables is well placed without the allegory. Have we counted? When do we notice what we have lost? What do we do to find what we have lost? Are we sure we've counted everything, and everyone?

## The Parable of the Lost Son

The parables of the Lost Sheep, the Lost Coin, and the Lost Son come as a set of three, and they are also connected by having basically the same outline: something is lost, there is a search, the lost item is found, and there is a celebration. They are also connected by their themes—loss, joy, and feasting. The first two parables end in feasting and celebration, but the third ends with the father and the older son out in the field. They are talking. We don't know how things end up between them. We aren't even completely sure by the end of the parable which son is the lost one. Perhaps they both are. Thus, the third parable offers particular challenges.

The parables thus follow a folkloric motif known as the "rule of three." In this storytelling, the first two examples set up the third. Two ugly and nasty stepsisters set up the kind and lovely Cinderella. Two pigs who do not know about engineering set up the third pig, who can build a house that will withstand a wolf's huffing and puffing. And the parables of the Lost Sheep and the Lost Coin set up the variation on the theme, the parable of the Lost Son.

The parable starts out like so many other stories before it: "There was a man who had two sons." This may sound familiar from tales in the Old Testament. Adam was a man who had two sons, Cain and Abel. Abraham had two sons, Ishmael and Isaac. And Isaac had twin sons, Esau and Jacob. We are used to this kind of story, and we know the plot line. We expect the older son to engage in evil or stupid actions, and we expect the younger son to emerge as clever, righteous, responsible, and the appropriate successor to his father. In this parable, however, the younger son turns out to be "prodigal," that is, wasteful and reckless. He does not match up at all with those earlier younger sons: Abel, Isaac, Jacob, and so on. This is the parable's first surprise.

Next, the younger son asks his father for his part of the inheritance. Today, his question might seem rude; it might seem as if he is treating his father as if the father is already dead. However, his question was not rude or unexpected in his own historical context. Very rich fathers were known to give their younger sons substantial sums so that the sons could make their way in the world. This distribution of property was not, for rich people, uncommon in those times.

The father does not admonish the son. He sees nothing wrong with the young man's question. Rather he gives him half of his property. Some might think it is the father who is here being prodigal!

The younger son then heads out on a journey, leaves home and so cuts off his network of support, and wastes the money on a life of excess. Jesus does not tell us that he "sinned"; sin and stupidity or irresponsibility are not the same thing. Once he has spent all the money, he falls victim to a famine and takes a job feeding pigs. Contrary to what many interpreters claim, this job is not meant to suggest that the son is violating purity laws. He is starving; he does what he has to do. He is in a Gentile area, it is clear, but that wasn't much of a problem to most Jews. The problem in this part of the parable is not being unclean. It is being hungry and alone.

Coming to his senses, the younger son makes a plan to go home and speak with his father. For those who want to interpret this parable as being about repenting and forgiving, this would be the repentance part. Yet Jesus says nothing here about whether the son actually repented. He simply says that the young man "came to himself." It sounds like the light bulb, or the oil lamp, went on over his head. Perhaps he did repent, but of what? What sin did he commit? Wasting one's money may be foolish, but it is not sinful.

Other interpreters see his comment as the trickery part—his words might be empty and constructed to get his way with his father, again. In other parables and indeed throughout the Bible, when characters are thinking to themselves (having an "interior monologue"), they are often up to no good.

We don't find out the result of the younger son's rehearsed words, because his father spots him coming, feels compassion for him, runs out to meet him, and showers him with kisses. This is no surprise, because why would we expect the father to do any less? The compassion he feels is the same as that felt by the Good Samaritan (Luke 10:33), and by Jesus when he sees the funeral procession of the widow's son (7:13), whom he raises. It is the sense that someone who is thought to be dead might become alive again.

Some commentators lean toward anti-Jewish interpretations when they suggest that the father was acting out of character, that Jewish fathers were usually distant or angry. There is no precedent for this in the Bible or in any other early Jewish book. In the Gospels, Jewish fathers provide bread for their children and seek healing for them. The father in this parable does not need to overcome an anti-Jewish stereotype in order to look commendable. His running to his son is not surprising: that is what parents do when children, gone and feared lost, return. His compassionate actions stand on their own. He doesn't need to hear any apology from his son. Instead, he calls for a new robe, a ring, sandals, and a dinner: the grain-fed calf or, traditionally, the "fatted calf."

The father is not concerned with his son's sincerity or repentance, just as the shepherd isn't looking for a repentant sheep, or the woman for a repentant coin. He rejoices that his son is home, he is basically back from the dead, and he adorns him with all the family's finest accessories.

However, remember that the parable starts out, "a man had *two* sons." Where is the older brother? Why isn't he invited to the party? Have we forgotten about him? If we determine that the parable is about the "Prodigal Son," then we have failed to count the *two* sons. The father has also failed to count.

The parable turns now to this older son, who is working in the fields. He asks a servant what's going on, learns that his brother is the reason for the extravagant party, and becomes angry. We might feel sorry for him. He is not a conventional angry older brother: he is not like Cain, who murders Abel; like Ishmael who, according to the angel, is "a wild ass of a man" (Genesis 16:12); or like Esau, who threatened to murder Jacob. He is simply an older brother, doing everything expected of him, and overlooked by his father. In the other two parables, the sheep owner and the woman summon their friends to the celebration when they find what is lost. But in this case, no one, including a number of readers, even notices that the brother is missing. That he feels slighted and ignored is no surprise.

Now the father realizes that the older son is missing. He goes out to plead with him, or comfort him. Like the sheep owner and woman before him, he needs to find what is lost and make his family complete. But his son is no sheep or coin. He is a human being, and his being "lost" to his father is more than a matter of physical misplacement.

The older son erupts with the unfairness of having been so loyal and obedient only to see his younger, prodigal brother rewarded for his recklessness with beautiful accessories and the celebration with all the friends and neighbors. Instead of using inclusive family language, like the prodigal, the servant, and the father ("this son of mine," "Father," "your brother"), the older brother distances himself. He refers to "this son of yours" as he details his outrage. He complains that the younger brother was associating with prostitutes, although Jesus did not make this point explicit. Perhaps the older brother is imagining what the younger brother did, and he is not kind in his imaginings.

There are a number of ways interpreters read the older son. A number of Christian readers have seen the older brother as representing "the Jews" or the Pharisees, and as suggesting that divine love has to be earned. They see "works righteousness" in the older brother's desire to be rewarded for his obedience rather than just experiencing the love and graciousness of his father. The problem here is that Judaism does not teach "works righteousness." To the contrary, those early Jews, like all Jews, do not follow Torah (the Law) in order to earn God's love. They already know they have this love, which is why God gave them the Torah in the first place. They follow Torah as a *response* to that initial love.

These readings that see the older brother as "the Jews" and his loyalty to his father as a sign of "works righteousness" see the parable as an allegory with the father representing God, the older brother representing recalcitrant and law-obsessed Jews, and the younger brother representing the new Christian family. But first-century Jews would never have come up with this interpretation. They would have seen an angry older brother whose father forgot to invite him to the party. As we have seen, parables are not allegories, and sometimes a family is just a family.

Finally, the father replies. "Son," he says (and the Greek word here is *teknon*, meaning, literally, "child" and with a possible sense of "beloved child"), "you are always with me, and all that is mine is yours." Legally, this statement is correct, because the father divided his property between the two sons. But the father continues: we still need to rejoice because your brother was dead and brought back to life, and he was lost but now he is found. The father is tender here, and he cares, deeply, for both of his children.

And allegorical readings casting the father as God and the older brother as the problematic Pharisees fall apart at this point. A brother was missing; the family was not whole. It is the older brother who is the subject of the father's search, and his attempt, through his words, to find and draw close. The younger brother who had been missing has returned, and in his father's eyes, he is brought back to life. Celebration is in store for everyone.

What happens next? Does the older son go to the party? What will the brothers' relationship look like when the father dies and his remaining property goes to the older son? The parable issues a challenge about families. "The parable shows us that indulgence does not buy love," Levine writes, "but withholding can stifle it." She observes that we search desperately when our families are not whole, and that while sheep and coins are relatively easy to find, children might be less so. And what to make of the prodigal? Levine doesn't trust him. He might seem humble and repentant when the story ends, but what will time tell? What about all the money he squandered?

If we leave out our tendency to read repentance and forgiveness into this parable, it does something more profound. Then the message becomes about what to do when one is lost. What if the lost one is right there in your home, like the older brother? Do what it takes to find him and celebrate his return. Don't wait for apologies or the ability to forgive. They may never come. Look for reconciliation.

And remember that what happens in the family extends out to the world. When we look around us, who do we find is lost? When we count among our families and communities, who is missing? Searching—for sheep, coins, or people—is work, but in the searching, there is also the finding and the potential to bring ourselves back to wholeness.

Do we count? Do we make sure everyone *feels* counted?

## QUESTIONS FOR REFLECTION

1.   Before reading this chapter, did you understand that the parables of the Lost Sheep, the Lost Coin, and the Lost Son were about repentance and forgiveness? Why or why not? Can they be not only about repentance and forgiveness, but also about our own responsibilities to make everyone feel counted?

2. How did reading alternate titles for the parables affect how you interpreted them?

3. Where is the challenge in these three parables? How do you find yourself challenged by these stories?

4. Were you taught to read the parable of the Lost Sheep as an allegory? If so, what did you learn that each element represented?

5. What have you lost in your life? Have you ever lost something that you would go to any lengths to find?

6. What have you learned about the parable of the Lost Son in your Christian education? Can you remember the interpretations you heard in Sunday school or sermons?

7. Why do you think the younger son wanted to take his inheritance and leave home?

8. What caused the younger brother's problems: his own actions? how he was raised (was he spoiled)? his leaving home? his prodigal lifestyle? the famine? the failure of anyone to give him anything?

9. Do you think the younger brother was repentant, or was he merely saying what he hoped his father would want him to say? What do you think will happen to him? Should he take any responsibility for his actions?

10. What do you think about the father's actions? Should he have given his younger son the money? Was he at fault for failing immediately to invite his older son to the celebration?

11. With whom do you identify in the parable of the Lost Son? the father? the older (responsible) brother? the younger (irresponsible) brother? the neighbors? the slave? Why?

12. Levine suggests that the parable actually focuses on the older brother. He is the one who was not counted. Did you ever feel like the older brother? Were you

the responsible child in the family? Did you ever feel overlooked because of attention paid to the "baby" in the family or to the "problem child"?

13. Does this story make you think differently about Cain, Ishmael, Esau, and all those other older brothers? Are they also part of our family?

14. Why do you think Jesus tells this story? What point is he trying to get across?

15. Some interpretations of the parable of the Lost Son have the potential for anti-Judaism. What are examples, and why?

16. Luke 15 begins with, "Now all the tax collectors and sinners were coming near to listen to him. And the Pharisees and the scribes were grumbling and saying, 'This fellow welcomes sinners and eats with them'" (verses 1-2). Jesus responds by telling these three parables. Why do you think Luke sets up the parables this way?

## PERSONAL RESPONSE

Read the following excerpts from *Short Stories by Jesus: The Enigmatic Parables of a Controversial Rabbi*. Consider the questions that follow in the context of the parables discussed in this chapter and your own personal experience.

This parable [of the Lost Son] might even be read as resisting Luke's easy interpretations of repentance and forgiveness. In this household, no one has expressed sorrow at hurting another, and no one has expressed forgiveness. When it comes to families, there are factors other than repentance and forgiveness that hold us together.

- What might these other factors be?
- If this parable is not about repentance and forgiveness, what is it about?
- Are repentance and forgiveness necessary elements of a happy family? Why or why not?

Both Matthew and Luke have provided our parables with a context, and in so doing they have begun the process of interpretation. We do well to see what the parables might have meant prior to their reception as Matthew's "instruction for church leaders" and Luke's "we love tax collectors, but Pharisees not so much."

- We might regard Luke as a pastor or priest who puts his own interpretation on the parables, just as people do when they give sermons on biblical texts. Do you think we can disregard Luke's interpretation and come to our own conclusions? Why or why not?

The sheep and the coin were "lost" and then "found"; they were passive objects. It is their owners, who first lost, then found, then celebrated, who should be the focus of our attention. They had the problem, and they fixed it. Thus, when we turn to the third parable in Luke 15, we might want to pay attention to the father, who comes to realize what he has lost and desperately wants to find and celebrate.

- How would your understanding of these parables be different were they titled, "The Sheep Owner Who Lost His Sheep," "The Woman Who Lost Her Coin," and "The

Father Who Lost His Son(s)"? How does reading the parable of the Lost Son in light of the first two parables affect how you interpret it? Which is more important, what gets lost, or who loses it?

- Have you ever felt that you were overlooked (not counted), that you were taken for granted rather than acknowledged?
- Did you ever feel resentful that the people who created problems, of whatever sort, got more attention than those who did what was expected of them? Is resentment a bad response? What did you do about this feeling?
- Levine emphasizes the importance of counting. Do we make sure that everyone we know—in our families, our churches, our classes, our places of employment—feels "counted"?
- In another context, Levine has discussed these three parables and the importance of counting at Nashville's maximum-security prison, where she often teaches classes. One of her insider students said, quietly, to her, "We are counted six times a day." How do we make sure that when we count people, we do so with dignity rather than just treating people as numbers or statistics?

## Session 2

# The Good Samaritan

### THE PARABLE

*Just then a lawyer stood up to test Jesus. "Teacher,"
he said, "what must I do to inherit eternal life?" He
said to him, "What is written in the law? What do
you read there?" He answered, "You shall love the
Lord your God with all your heart, and with all your
soul, and with all your strength, and with all your
mind; and your neighbor as yourself." And he said to
him, "You have given the right answer; do this, and
you will live."*

*But wanting to justify himself, he asked Jesus, "And
who is my neighbor?" Jesus replied, "A man was going
down from Jerusalem to Jericho, and fell into the
hands of robbers, who stripped him, beat him, and
went away, leaving him half dead. Now by chance
a priest was going down that road; and when he*

*saw him, he passed by on the other side. So likewise
a Levite, when he came to the place and saw him,
passed by on the other side. But a Samaritan while
traveling came near him; and when he saw him, he
was moved with pity. He went to him and bandaged
his wounds, having poured oil and wine on them.
Then he put him on his own animal, brought him
to an inn, and took care of him. The next day he
took out two denarii, gave them to the innkeeper,
and said, 'Take care of him; and when I come back,
I will repay you whatever more you spend.' Which of
these three, do you think, was a neighbor to the man
who fell into the hands of the robbers?" He said, "The
one who showed him mercy." Jesus said to him, "Go
and do likewise."*

*Luke 10:25-37*

## CHAPTER SUMMARY

The term "good Samaritan" has become synonymous with
anyone who does good deeds or performs acts of charity. There are
Good Samaritan hospitals, the Samaritans international charity
organization, and even a Good Samaritan Donkey Sanctuary.
The parable is so well known that people in various nonreligious
contexts invoke the phrase "good Samaritan" to describe
outstanding feats of goodness. This focus on the Samaritan's good
deed, while not inappropriate, domesticates the story. That focus
makes the story about helping others, or even going the extra mile.
Such readings are not incorrect, but they are insufficient. Jesus's
parable is much more profound, and we can find this profundity
when we hear the parable in its first-century context. How did
Jesus's original audience hear this parable?

The parable is introduced in Jesus's reply to a lawyer who asked him, "What must I do to inherit eternal life?" (Luke 10:25). Elsewhere in Luke (although not always elsewhere in the New Testament), lawyers are not among the righteous, so readers might get the idea here that this lawyer might not be a stand-up guy. There are a few further clues for this. The lawyer calls Jesus "Teacher" (10:25). This address suggests that the lawyer doesn't fully understand or respect who Jesus really is. If he did, he would have called Jesus "Lord."

Even more telling, his question to Jesus is a test, quite a negative thing, according to Luke. Earlier, it was Satan who tested Jesus (Luke 4:2; translated "tempted" in the NRSV), so the lawyer is in the Devil's role. Finally, the language the lawyer uses regarding actions required for eternal life suggests that he is looking for one item to check off his to-do list. He is not making a sincere query about how to live in a righteous way. All in all, the lawyer has asked an illegitimate question to which, as far as the details go, he already knows the answer.

Then, Jesus answers a question with a question. "What is written in the law? What do you read there?" Jesus asks (10:26). He pitches the query back to the lawyer. "The law" refers to the Torah, or the first five books of the Old Testament (Genesis, Exodus, Leviticus, Numbers, and Deuteronomy). But there's not a lot in the Torah about eternal life or life after death. These books are much more concerned with how to live in the present. Their concern is how one loves one's neighbor as oneself, not how one gets into heaven.

In his reply to the lawyer, Jesus is asking not just what is written, but how the lawyer interprets what is written. His question implies that the lawyer is literate. That was not the case with many people in the first century. Today, in the industrialized West, we tend to forget that there was a time when people could not read, and this is still true in some places today.

The lawyer answers Jesus's question with two verses from the Torah: "You shall love the Lord your God with all your heart, and with all your soul, and with all your strength, and with all your mind; and your neighbor as yourself" (Luke 10:27; the lawyer's response is a combination of two Torah verses: Leviticus 19:18 and Deuteronomy 6:5). The lawyer was aware of the commandments; whether he fully understood them is another question.

Jesus congratulates the lawyer for getting the right answer. "Do this, and you will live," he advises (Luke 10:28). But the lawyer won't let the matter drop. He's apparently not about to go live a life of righteousness and love. So he asks another question: "And who is my neighbor?" (10:29). It's actually a good question. We could conclude that "to ask 'Who is my neighbor' is a polite way of asking, 'Who is *not* my neighbor?' or 'Who does not deserve my love?'"

However, Jewish teaching never restricted love only to those who are fellow Jews. Leviticus 19:18b states, "you shall love your neighbor as yourself: I am the LORD." But Leviticus goes on also to mandate, "The alien who resides with you shall be to you as the citizen among you; you shall love the alien as yourself, for you were aliens in the land of Egypt: I am the LORD your God" (Leviticus 19:34). Both neighbor and alien or foreigner are to be loved.

It is important to maintain both categories. The neighbor is a fellow Jew, with the same rights and responsibilities as other Jews. The stranger is not a Jew: the stranger has different rights and responsibilities, but the stranger must also be loved.

Jesus's answer to the lawyer's query, "Who is my neighbor?" is not a discourse in what constitutes "neighbor" but a parable. Jesus sees, writes Amy-Jill Levine, that "Everyone deserves that love—

local or alien, Jews or gentile, terrorist or rapist, everyone." Luke's depiction of Jesus makes it clear that love is not to be restricted, no matter whether one is a neighbor or a stranger.

The parable begins, "A man was going down from Jerusalem to Jericho" (10:30), or, as Levine translates, "Some person." The man gets no more description than that. He could be anyone (or everyone). Speculation about his identity, or the identities and motives of the robbers, is simply that—speculation. He is simply a man who finds himself in a ditch, a victim of a violent crime. The road from Jerusalem to Jericho was a notoriously difficult and dangerous one; most listeners would have known this. The stage is set, the crime takes place, and the man is left on the road "half dead."

Next in the parable, a priest avoids our victim by crossing on the other side of the road. Then a Levite does the same thing. Who were these men, and what would Jesus's listeners have heard? Some contend that the priest and the Levite are both members of the elite priestly class, but there is nothing to suggest this. As Levine remarks, "Stereotypes get in the way." Some priests and many Levites were, in fact, among the poorer members of society. For priests, we might think about John the Baptist's father, a village priest living in the hill country.

Many interpreters also assume that the priest and the Levite avoid the wounded man because of concerns about ritual purity. Coming in contact with a corpse might have rendered them ritually unclean. But, as Levine shows, this interpretation is incorrect. Concerns about purity are irrelevant here; at the very least, the two are required to aid the man in order to confirm whether he is dead. Without knowing exactly why the priest and the Levite step aside, we can only guess about their reasons for passing him by. Levine quotes Martin Luther King Jr., for the best explanation as to why these two men refused to stop and render aid. King remarks that it's possible that the priest and the Levite were afraid. Maybe the first thing they thought was, "If I stop to help this man, what will happen to me?" But then the Good Samaritan thought something different. He thought, "If I do not stop to help this man, what will happen to him?"

We can't know precisely the motives of the priest and the Levite, but Levine posits that Dr. King has the right idea—they were only concerned for themselves. But if there weren't religious concerns driving their behavior, why make the characters in the story a priest and a Levite? Remember the "rule of three"? In the parables of the lost items, the first two stories set up the third. The same thing is happening here. Upon hearing that a priest and a Levite passed by the injured man, what would Jesus's audience have expected?

They would have anticipated a third man, and his identity would have been obvious. The next man to come along—and the one who would ultimately help the man—would be an Israelite. The priestly line descends from Aaron, the brother of Moses. Levites descend from Levi, Aaron's ancestor and the third son of Jacob. And all other Jews come through Jacob's other children. They are Israelites. Anyone who knows anything about Judaism—that is, Jesus's initial audience—could have seen this coming: the third person *must* be an Israelite. But Jesus is telling a parable here, and what happens next is a shock. The next person who comes along is a Samaritan. Although a number of readers today think of Samaritans as the oppressed minority, that was not the case in Jesus's own context. "In modern terms," Levine writes, "this would be like going from Larry and Moe to Osama bin Laden."

Where Jesus gave few details about the man in the ditch, the priest, and the Levite, he goes into great detail about the Samaritan's actions. The dismissive actions of the first two are reversed by the Samaritan's display of compassion (this is the same Greek word as we saw in the parable of the Lost Son [15:20]), his attention to the injured man's wounds, and his willingness to stop his journey and take care of a stranger.

Many interpreters want to see the Samaritan as an oppressed figure, or a stand-in for minority groups. But we would come closer to Jesus's original audience if we thought of the Samaritan as the enemy, or the one doing the oppressing. Early listeners might be appalled by the idea of getting help from a Samaritan. Those first-century Jews, thinking about a Samaritan coming near, would have feared that this Samaritan would murder them, or rape them. Some geographical and historical context is helpful here.

- After the twelve-tribe united monarchy under David split in two, the Southern Kingdom (Judah) had its capital in Jerusalem. The Northern Kingdom (Israel or Ephraim) eventually made its capital at the city of Samaria.
- The Northern Kingdom was conquered by the Assyrians in 722 BCE, and many of its people were deported.
- The Assyrians then moved other people into the emptied places, such as Samaria, in place of the people whom they exiled (2 Kings 17:24). The resulting group was called the Samaritans.
- Babylon conquered Assyria and then, in 587 BCE, the Southern Kingdom, Judah, and sent many into exile in Babylon.
- In 538 BCE, Cyrus of Persia, who had conquered Babylon, repatriated the exiles from Judea.
- Jews who came back were planning to rebuild their Temple. Over these construction plans, a new hostility between Jews returning from Babylon and Samaritans developed.
- Around 388 BCE, the Samaritans built their own temple on Mt. Gerizim.

- In 333 BCE, Samaria was rebuilt as a Greek city, and hostilities with the Jews in the south continued.
- In 128 BCE, the Jewish king John Hyrcanus burned down the Samaritan Temple on Mt. Gerizim.
- From the late sixth century BCE until the time of Jesus, Jews and Samaritans were at odds, with each claiming to be the true descendants of Abraham, to have the true understanding of Torah, to have the correct priesthood, and to have the right kind of worship in the right place.
- Samaritans call themselves *Shomrim* or Shamerim, which means "guardians" or "observers" of the Law.
- Samaritans and Jews each think the other has gone off track and gotten it wrong as far as biblical interpretation is concerned. Samaritans don't believe the Prophets and the Writings should have been added to the Bible. That is, the first five books (the Torah) should be the beginning and end of Scripture. Their text of these books is, today, called the Samaritan Pentateuch.

The Gospel of John reflects this enmity between Jews and Samaritans in the story of Jesus asking the woman at the well for a drink. John reports, "Jews do not share things in common with Samaritans" (4:9). And according to Matthew, Jesus tells his followers, "Enter no town of the Samaritans" (10:5). Luke describes, just one chapter before our parable, how Jesus is refused hospitality in a Samaritan village (9:52-53). Sources outside the Bible confirm that Samaritans and Jews were hostile. Josephus (37–ca. 100), a Jewish historian, describes direct Samaritan attacks on Jews. There was no love lost between Samaritans and Jews, and Jesus's listeners would have been acutely aware of this. There was no oppressor-oppressed relationship between Jews and Samaritans; the antagonism was mutual.

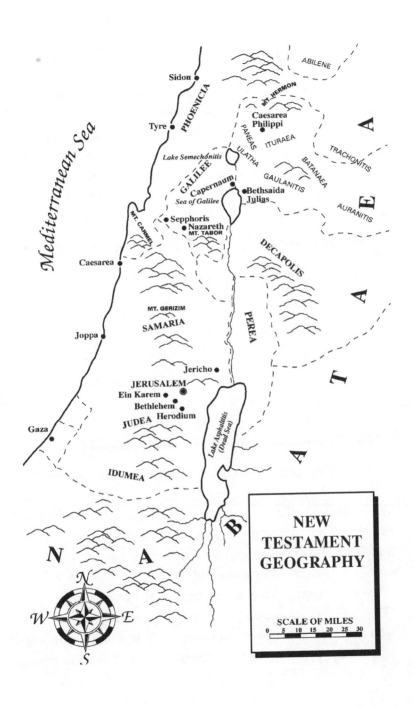

Mediterranean Sea

Sidon

Tyre

PHOENICIA

ABILENE

MT. HERMON

Caesarea
Philippi

PANEAS

ITURAEA

TRACHONITIS

Lake Semechonitis

ULATHA

GALILEE

Capernaum

Sea of Galilee

Bethsaida
Julias

GAULANITIS

BATANAEA

AURANITIS

Sepphoris

Nazareth

MT. TABOR

MT. CARMEL

DECAPOLIS

Caesarea

MT. GERIZIM

SAMARIA

PEREA

Joppa

Jericho

JERUSALEM

Ein Karem

Bethlehem

Herodium

JUDEA

Lake Asphaltitis
(Dead Sea)

Gaza

IDUMEA

N        A

T

A

B

A

NEW
TESTAMENT
GEOGRAPHY

N

W        E

S

SCALE OF MILES

0    5   10  15  20  25  30

But it is the Samaritan, the enemy, who stops to help. Indeed, the Samaritan stops and does much more than listeners might expect. He goes even further; he takes the injured man to an inn and puts up his own money (two denarii) for the care of the man. He promises to return and reimburse any additional expenses. This verse establishes that the Samaritan is no social outcast. Clearly, he has money, the ability to travel, and some negotiating skills. Perhaps, when he promises to return, he is actually issuing a threat: "I'm coming back, so you'd better take care of this man!"

---

**The Samaritan's offer of long-term care demonstrates that love of neighbor is something that is ongoing. The Samaritan trusts the innkeeper, and the wounded man trusts the Samaritan. This kind of trust is essential.**

---

The parable is not about prejudice and marginalized people; it is about hatred between people who have similar resources. The Samaritan's offer of long-term care demonstrates that love of neighbor is something that is ongoing. The Samaritan trusts the innkeeper, and the wounded man trusts the Samaritan. This kind of trust is essential. The parable ends here.

Now the text returns to the conversation with the lawyer. "Which of these three, do you think, was a neighbor to the man who fell into the hands of the robbers?" Jesus asks (10:36). The lawyer can't even say the word "Samaritan," and so he answers,

"The one who showed him mercy" (10:37). Jesus responds that the lawyer should go and do likewise. Note that he doesn't say, go and *be* likewise. The emphasis is on action; go and *do*. Love of God and love of neighbor are to be enacted. What does the lawyer do upon hearing this parable? Luke doesn't tell us. What remains is only what *we* will do with the message we have heard.

Levine points out that the parable sends a profound message about how we regard others with whom we are in conflict. She writes, "Can we finally agree that it is better to acknowledge the humanity and the potential to do good in the enemy, rather than to choose death?" Imagine the potential of being able to bind up our enemies' wounds, or to have them do the same to us. This is how Jesus's audience would have heard and been forced to consider the message of the parable of the Good Samaritan.

Levine considers this parable in its most current, literal sense. Today Samaria is called the West Bank, Occupied Palestine, or Greater Israel. What if the traveler is an Israeli Jew on his way from Jerusalem to Jericho, and he is attacked by robbers and left half-dead in a ditch? And then two people pass by who should help, a Jewish medic from the Israeli Defense Force and a missionary from the Presbyterian Church U.S.A. But the person who actually has compassion for the traveler is a Palestinian Muslim, a Hamas sympathizer. Hamas is a political party that looks for the destruction of Israel.

This would be the parable of the "Good Hamas Member." As Levine reflects, "If people in the Middle East could picture this, we might have a better vision for choosing life."

## QUESTIONS FOR REFLECTION

1. Before you read this chapter, what did the phrase "good Samaritan" suggest to you?

2. How did you first learn about this parable? What was the lesson of the story?

3. What do you think of the lawyer's questions? How are they similar to the questions we ask of religion today? Is attaining eternal life the whole point of the parable, or of Jesus's teachings in general, or does this parable, and Jesus, point to something more?

4. How does knowing that Jews and Samaritans had a contentious relationship change the message of the story for you?

5. Levine points out that there are hospitals and charity organizations with the name "Samaritan," and even "Good Samaritan" animal rescue groups. What images are these groups invoking? Why do you think "Samaritan" has become such a powerful symbol? Does the symbol still make sense once you know the original context of the parable?

6. Could the title "Good Samaritan" be offensive? How would you feel about a story entitled "The Good Muslim," "The Good Methodist," or "The Good Jew"?

7. In the parable, the Samaritan had compassion for the man in the ditch (Luke 10:33). How does knowing that the identities of these two men were in conflict expand or complicate that compassion?

8. Today, readers typically identify with the Samaritan. Jesus's original audience would not have wanted to find themselves identifying with a Samaritan. The church fathers who first offered commentary on the parable called it "the parable of the man who fell among the robbers." How does our identification

with the various figures in the parable change the
impact of the parable?

9. One message of the parable might be that it is important
   to help others no matter who they are. What other
   messages might Jesus's audience have heard?

10. Jesus tells this parable in response to the lawyer's
    questions, "What must I do to inherit eternal life?"
    (Luke 10:25) and "Who is my neighbor?" (Luke 10:29).
    Are these good questions? How does the parable address
    each of these questions?

11. Some interpreters find that the priest and the Levite
    do not stop to help because they are obeying purity
    laws that prohibit them from touching a corpse. What
    reasons does Levine present to counter this view? Why
    do you think the priest and the Levite do not stop to help
    the man?

12. Is the parable a warning against prejudice? Why or why
    not? If so, what message might the story give about
    prejudice?

13. What modern equivalents would you cast in this parable
    to replace the Samaritan? What about the priest and the
    Levite? How could you make this story pack a punch in
    today's world?

14. Levine recasts the parable in a Middle Eastern context:
    Samaria is the West Bank, the man in the ditch is
    an Israeli Jew, and the passers-by are a Jewish medic
    and a Christian peace worker. The one who comes
    to help, ultimately, is a member of Hamas. How does
    this modern context change your interpretation of the
    parable?

## Personal Response

Read the following excerpts from *Short Stories by Jesus*. Consider the questions that follow in the context of the parables discussed in this chapter and your own personal experience.

> Both priest and Levite should have stopped to help. The audience, surprised at this lack of compassion, would have presumed both that the third person would be an Israelite and that he would help.
>
> However, Jesus is telling a parable, and parables never go the way one expects. Instead of the anticipated Israelite, the person who stops to help is a Samaritan. In modern terms, this would be like going from Larry and Moe to Osama bin Laden.

- How do you relate to this story when you find out that the Good Samaritan is actually a mortal enemy?
- Do you make a place for unexpected events to change your relationships?
- Who are your "enemies" today?
- Would you expect them to help you or to pass you by?
- Would you stop to help your enemy if he or she were wounded?

Levine quotes Martin Luther King Jr. for the best explanation as to why these two men refused to stop and render aid. King remarks that it's possible that the priest and the Levite were afraid. Maybe the first thing they thought was, "If I stop to help this man, what will happen to me?" But then the Good Samaritan thought something different. He thought, "If I do not stop to help this man, what will happen to him?"

- Can you think of a current event or other present-day example that illustrates this principle?
- When in your life has care for another person come before the potential consequences to yourself?
- How often do you decide what to do based on the consequences for you?
- How does reversing the question prompt you to enact the instruction to love God and neighbor offered just before the parable?

Those who want to kill you may be the only ones who will save you.

- Reflect on this statement in light of the parable of the Good Samaritan. Do you think this is true?
- What does this mean for our relationships with our neighbors—and our enemies?
- Levine cites 2 Chronicles 28 as an example of this idea. Can you think of any other biblical stories that illustrate this concept?
- Have you experienced anything in your life that supports this statement?
- What examples from current events demonstrate this lesson?

# Session 3

# The Pearl of Great Price

## THE PARABLE

*"Again, the kingdom of heaven is like a merchant in search of fine pearls; on finding one pearl of great value, he went and sold all that he had and bought it."*

*Matthew 13:45-46*

## CHAPTER SUMMARY

Scholars typically interpret the parable of the Pearl of Great Price as an allegory for Christian discipleship. In this case, turning the decoder ring reveals that the merchant is the model disciple, and the pearl is the good news, or the gospel. The merchant not only invests in this good news, but he sacrifices everything for it. For some pastors, the interpretation is still an allegory, but Jesus is both the subject and object, the searcher and the pearl himself.

Still others see the pearl as the church, purchased with the blood of Christ.

All of these interpretations make sense, especially when we read the parable as divorced from its literary and historical context. No one in Jesus's initial audience would conclude that the pearl had anything to do with Jesus's blood, because they did not even know that he would be crucified. Turning parables into allegories doesn't get to what they would have meant to their original audiences. You need the special decoder ring to understand an allegory; the original audiences wouldn't have had access to such a key. Further, allegorical readings don't usually present a challenge, and this is what we have come to expect from parables.

A more historical read of this parable resists the allegory and concentrates instead on the merchant and the pearl, the seeming foolishness of the merchant's actions, and questions of "surprise, identity, and ultimate concern." What do we consider so important that we will give up everything we own—even our own identities, as the merchant is no longer a merchant once he buys the pearl!—to possess or protect it?

Amy-Jill Levine's translation of the parable reveals a subtle point in the original Greek. The NRSV reads, "The kingdom of heaven is like a merchant in search of fine pearls" (Matthew 13:45). Levine's more literal translation renders, "The kingdom of heaven is like a man [Greek: *anthropos*], a merchant, seeking fine pearls" (13:45). This man is a person, someone with whom we can all identify. Secondarily, he is a merchant.

In Greek, the word for merchant (*emporos*) has the meaning of wholesaler, or, as Levine says, "one who markets through agents items consumers do not need at prices they cannot afford." In contrast to the man in the preceding parable (13:44) who happens to find a treasure in a field, the merchant is already in search of fine things. Today, we generally think positively of merchants. In the biblical context, this was not the case, so comparing the kingdom to a merchant would have raised some eyebrows. Merchants, *emporoi*—and the whole enterprise of trade, *emporia*—have negative connotations both in the Bible and in antiquity. For example, when Jesus gets upset in the Temple, he cries, "Stop making my Father's house a marketplace!" (John 2:16; the Greek word used here is *emporiou*). Throughout the New Testament and the Septuagint (the Greek translation of the Old Testament), this family of words is used almost exclusively with negative connotations. By saying that the kingdom of heaven is like a merchant, Jesus has at the very least caught his listeners' attention.

For those who want to interpret the parable as an allegory, the pearl—since it is the most desirable thing one could have—must symbolize Christ, or the gospel, or the kingdom. But the parable actually says that the kingdom of heaven is compared to the *merchant*, not the pearl. Perhaps this is part of the parable's challenge? In addition, pearls aren't just another type of pretty jewelry. The merchant is searching specifically for "fine pearls," not just any type of jewel. At this time, pearls were the finest jewel one could imagine. No common person would have access to pearls.

There are certain details about pearls that are worth noting. First, pearls come from oysters, which are not kosher. However, although shellfish is, like pork, avoided by Jews who follow the dietary regulations set out in the book of Leviticus, there is no law against wearing a pearl. Perhaps because of the dietary laws, pearls aren't mentioned in the Old Testament. Second, pearls come from living creatures, unlike most other jewels. Finally, the creation of pearls is a matter of self-protection, and perhaps suffering, for the oyster. Pearls do show up elsewhere in the New Testament—"Do not throw your pearls before swine" (Matthew 7:6); "Women should dress...not...with gold, pearls, or expensive clothes" (1 Timothy 2:9); Babylon "the great city...adorned with gold, with jewels, and with pearls!" (Revelation 18:16). For 1 Timothy, a pearl is just another outrageous accessory that inspires sin. Nowhere, except possibly in this parable, are pearls named as exquisite and precious, of singular value.

The merchant and the pearl both have negative connotations. We might also question the merchant's actions. He is actively seeking; he is "in search of fine pearls" (Matthew 13:45). He is not satisfied with how things are. He wants more precious items. We are not told if he wants to sell them or to keep them, but since he is a merchant, he is likely on the lookout for jewels to sell. Despite all the allegorical interpretations, he's just searching for pearls, not a way of life, not Christ, not salvation. He gets one pearl of great value, and he sells everything he has to get it. This is what the merchant is up to.

But, as Levine points out, that merchant may not be the sharpest tack in the box. He starts off searching for fine pearls, but he stops after finding one. He can't go on in his business, since he's given up everything he owns. The Greek phrase meaning "all that he had" suggests that the merchant did more than just liquidate his supply of goods. Instead, he sold everything he owned, his home, his food, his clothing, his family's belongings and provisions. He gave up all of this to satisfy his great desire. But once he has this pearl of great value, what will he do? Surely it is a beautiful object, but it cannot feed, shelter, or clothe him. He was able to find the pearl, but it is up in the air whether it was an act of common sense to sell everything else to buy it. This is a huge risk, and there's nothing to suggest that the pearl was a good investment, or an investment at all. The parable says nothing about his selling this pearl. So, now what?

Matters are even more peculiar. The merchant has not only acquired the pearl, he has abandoned his identity. Having sold off everything, he is no longer a merchant. He redefines himself, and we see him differently as well. What is he now? And how do we interpret this parable?

---

In the end, we might stop trying to identify exactly what, for Jesus, that pearl represents. Instead, we do well to pay attention to what the merchant does. He is able to recognize that which is his ultimate concern, the most important thing in his life.

---

Levine offers a few possibilities that have arisen over the years. In an early attempt to domesticate the parable, the *Gospel of Thomas* (an early non-canonical gospel) offers an allegorical reading: the pearl is special knowledge that must be sought. Such a reading creates a perfect allegory, though, and the parable loses its ability to challenge and provoke. It also suggests that Jesus is peddling some secret knowledge available only to some people. Contemporary critics offer this approach: true disciples are those who sacrifice everything to be a part of God's valuable kingdom. Or, as Levine puts it, "The merchant is the true disciple, his goods are sacrificial offerings used to aid a fellow disciple, and the pearl is the railway ticket, the gratitude of the recipient, or whatever is seen to promote Christian virtue." However, we don't have any reason to think that the merchant has *sacrificed* anything; he simply sold everything he had. We don't see that he is suffering from the loss.

Others insist that the parable has nothing to do with economics at all. Perhaps the valuable pearl stands in for knowledge of scripture or hope for God's kingdom. However, on its surface, this parable has all kinds of economic imagery. Allegorical readings that insist that Jesus is not talking about economics sidestep the parable's primary content. Finally, some commentators see a quest for detachment, or freedom from worldly concerns, and this is what the merchant achieves by recognizing the valuable thing and selling everything else. But if we detach ourselves from worldly concerns, what are we saying about our families, or our responsibility to others or to the earth?

In the end, we might stop trying to identify exactly what, for Jesus, that pearl represents. Instead, we do well to pay attention to what the merchant does. He is able to recognize that which is his ultimate concern, the most important thing in his life. The parable asks: What is worth so much that we will sell all we have—that we will do *anything*—to obtain it? The merchant finds something he wasn't searching for (one precious pearl instead of "fine pearls"). He gives up his possessions and his very identity to own the precious pearl that he desired. Once he spends everything on the pearl, he is no longer a merchant. This is the parable's challenge.

Most would agree that the merchant acts recklessly. But he does what he desires. He has the courage to change his life mid-course, because he has found something that speaks to him, or calls to him. We want to know what is so special about this pearl, because something must be. What is important to him may not be important to us; what makes perfect sense to him may make no sense to us. And so the parable challenges again.

The parable raises questions about our own desires. Why are we constantly seeking the next thing, the better thing, the bucket list, the heart's desire? Levine reads the parable in this way: knowing what our one precious pearl is cancels out all other desires. Will we know it when we see it? The merchant did. A further challenge comes when we ask ourselves whether we are willing to give everything for our ultimate concern, that is, that which we value above all else. "Are we willing to step aside from all we have to obtain what we want?" Can we take a step away from our present identity, perhaps an identity imposed on us by family or friends or circumstances, and become what we've always wanted to be? And finally, the parable challenges us to know what is of ultimate concern to our neighbors. How can we follow the commandment to "love your neighbor as yourself" (Leviticus 19:18; Jesus repeats this commandment in Matthew 19:19 and elsewhere) if we do not know what is the most important thing in our neighbor's life?

Levine describes her experience discussing the parable with graduate students. One woman who had been denied access to pursuing a degree described the Ph.D. as her pearl of great price. She gave up everything, her status, her financial security, her very identity as a professional, in order to return to school and follow her dream. Levine also teaches at a maximum-security prison in Nashville, where for the insider students, the pearls of great price are things like "freedom" and "safety." Is one person's pearl of great price something that others of us take for granted?

To live with kingdom-of-heaven values, we are called to prioritize our values and identify our ultimate concerns. Realizing that our pearl of great price may be our children, freedom from harm, an education, or the life we've always wanted, we might also realize that this demands of us a new way to live. If we find our pearl, can we stop being acquisitive, and will we know when enough is enough? If we know what our ultimate concern is, our pearl of great price, can we more easily focus on what really matters and so direct our attention in a more helpful way? If we can identify our pearl of great price, what does that identification say about us? For some people, the pearl is justice, compassion, family, or health. For others, however, it is money, beauty, fame, or power. How do we want to be known? The parable gives us a man who has a pearl. For what do we want to be known? The parable issues a number of forceful challenges, and this is what parables are supposed to do.

---

If we find our pearl, can we stop being acquisitive, and will we know when enough is enough? If we know what our ultimate concern is, our pearl of great price, can we more easily focus on what really matters and so direct our attention in a more helpful way?

---

## QUESTIONS FOR REFLECTION

1. How do we think of merchants today? What terms do we use? What are the associations with those terms? What comes to your mind when you think of merchants?
2. Levine shows that merchants and pearls could have negative connotations to Jesus's original audience. Why do you think Jesus chose to teach with items like this?
3. Does the merchant's decision to sell all that he has and buy one amazing pearl surprise you? What do you think

is behind his decision? Does it show good business sense? What would Jesus's original audience have thought of that decision?

4. Modern allegories of this parable cast the pearl as "the most desirable thing one could have," and so it symbolizes Christ or the gospel or the kingdom. What do such allegorical interpretations suggest, then, about the merchant and his search? Do you think allegories are helpful? Why or why not?

5. Do you own any pearls, or have you ever given pearls as a gift? What do you associate with pearls?

6. The merchant sells all his possessions—food, clothing, provisions for his family, *everything*—in order to buy the pearl. What do you think of his actions? What do you think Jesus is trying to say with this part of the story? Is the merchant's divestiture comparable to what Jesus calls his disciples to do? Is living the gospel the same thing as buying a pearl?

7. In Matthew's Gospel, another parable appears just before our story:

> *The kingdom of heaven is like treasure hidden in a field, which someone found and hid; then in his joy he goes and sells all that he has and buys that field.*
>
> *Matthew 13:44*

Does it change the meaning of the parable of the Pearl of Great Price to read it in light of this parable? How are the two stories different? How are they similar? Are the messages the same?

8. Levine has noted that titles matter. Does the title "The Pearl of Great Price" affect how you interpret this parable? After reading this chapter, what title(s) would you give this parable?

9. After the merchant finds the pearl, he gives up everything, including his identity. Without any possessions, he is no longer a merchant. He is a man with a pearl. Have you ever completely changed your occupation, living situation, or group of friends? What did it feel like to give up one circumstance for another?

10. The merchant becomes "a man with a pearl." By what title or object or activity would you want to be known? What is your ultimate concern?

11. The merchant sees the pearl and immediately sells everything in order to have the funds to buy it. Levine asks, "Will we know what we truly want when we see it?" Is there anything in your life that would be worth giving up everything for? Explain your response.

## PERSONAL RESPONSE

Read the following excerpts from *Short Stories by Jesus*. Consider the questions that follow in the context of the parable discussed in this chapter and your own personal experience.

Recognizing both the merchant's search for multiple pearls and his unexpected decision to purchase only one, we might find a reading that allows us to recognize what is of ultimate importance for ourselves as well as for our neighbors. Realizing that once the merchant obtains his pearl of utmost value, he is no longer a merchant, we might discover a challenge to our own identity.

- How does this parable challenge you?
- The merchant realizes that the pearl is of ultimate importance to him. What is of ultimate importance in your life? a person? a job? a piece of art? justice? compassion? love? money or beauty or power?

Pearls are formed when the oyster, to protect itself from a foreign object such as a grain of sand lodged between its mantle and shell, coats the object with nacre, the same substance that creates the expanding shell.

- How might this description of the formation of a pearl inform your interpretation of the parable?
- What, if any, symbolic value does this description lend to the valuable pearl?

Whether what [the merchant] does is risky or wise, foolhardy or dedicated, he has gained a pearl of enormous value. In the gaining, he has not only fulfilled a desire he did not know he had; he has also changed his identity. He had been looking for fine pearls, but he buys only one. By finding that pearl of ultimate worth, the merchant stops being a merchant. Thus he redefines himself, and we must see him anew as well. What is he? What do we make of his example? What does a former merchant "do" with a pearl? How do we locate ourselves in the parable?

- With whom do you identify in this parable? the merchant? the seller of the pearl? the merchant's family left behind?
- What do you imagine to be the fate of this merchant and his incredible pearl?
- What do you think is Jesus's point in telling this story?
- What is your pearl?

Our erstwhile merchant first raises questions of our own acquisitiveness. We are continually seeking, whether the object is fine pearls, a new job, another degree, or spiritual fulfillment.

- If this is true, what can we learn from this parable about our own searching and the ability to be content?
- Do you find yourself to be constantly reaching for the next thing?
- How do we know when enough is enough?

# Session 4

# The Mustard Seed

## THE PARABLE

*He also said, "With what can we compare the kingdom of God, or what parable will we use for it? It is like a mustard seed, which, when sown upon the ground, is the smallest of all the seeds on earth; yet when it is sown it grows up and becomes the greatest of all shrubs, and puts forth large branches, so that the birds of the air can make nests in its shade."*

*Mark 4:30-32*

*He put before them another parable: "The kingdom of heaven is like a mustard seed that someone took and sowed in his field; it is the smallest of all the seeds, but when it has grown it is the greatest of shrubs and becomes a tree, so that the birds of the air come and make nests in its branches."*

*Matthew 13:31-32*

*He said therefore, "What is the kingdom of God like? And to what should I compare it? It is like a mustard seed that someone took and sowed in the garden; it grew and became a tree, and the birds of the air made nests in its branches."*

*Luke 13:18-19*

## CHAPTER SUMMARY

The parable of the Mustard Seed appears in all three Synoptic (or "seen together") Gospels—Matthew, Mark, and Luke—each time with slightly different details. Because the stories vary—in Matthew, "someone took and sowed" the seed in a field (Matthew 13:31); Luke's original language suggests more of a "casting" or "tossing" of the seed in a garden (Luke 13:19)—it is difficult to know the exact substance of Jesus's original parable. Even so, biblical scholars have set forth so many "branches" of interpretation that, to use Amy-Jill Levine's metaphor, "the birds of heaven could build multiple nests and still have room for expansion."

Two main interpretations dominate: one focuses on the contrast between large and small, and the other looks at the symbolic value of mustard, the tree, the birds, and the branches. For example, some interpreters see in the smallness of the seed and the giant tree the amazing growth of the kingdom, or the church. Others see the birds as the Gentile nations gathered in the church. Still others see the seed growing as the church grows, inevitably. Or the seed grows as a symbol of eternal life in Christ, or even resurrection. More political views suggest that the mustard seed is a weed that threatens the garden (or the status quo), or that the mustard seed is violating the Jewish law that only one crop should be planted in a plot of land. Such readings give rise to anti-Jewish interpretations emphasizing the negative value of Jewish law, which cannot have been the message Jesus gave or his original audiences heard. Mustard seed is not, contrary to some uninformed interpreters, a symbol of impurity, and mustard is entirely kosher (as anyone eating a kosher hot dog with mustard can tell you, Levine points out). Other interpreters say that the mustard seed shows how the kingdom doesn't come with a big production, but rather arrives in a tiny seed. None of these interpretations is likely what Jesus's original audience heard, nor do they get at the challenge inherent in the parable of the Mustard Seed. In this chapter, Levine shows how the interpretive traditions around this parable are infected with anti-Judaism, then demonstrates "how the parable poses challenges to Jewish readers and at the same time treats distinct Jewish practices with respect."

First, mustard seed is not, as Jesus proclaims, "the smallest of all the seeds" (Mark 4:31; Matthew 13:32). Orchid seeds and cypress seeds are smaller than mustard seeds. Furthermore, mustard seeds do not grow into tall trees. Most mustard seeds grow into bushes. Jesus's point is not to teach a science lesson but to offer a parable, one that does make a contrast: a tiny seed grows into a tree (or bush) that makes a home for birds. No challenge so far. We can ascribe all kinds of symbols to the elements of this parable, but it's possible that the seed, tree, and birds are just that: a seed, a tree, and some birds making a home there.

Here is what we know: the mustard seed grows into a tree. Mark reports only a "shrub," Matthew describes a shrub that "becomes a tree," and Luke offers simply that the seed "became a tree." Here, interpreters try to figure out the exact words Jesus might have used. However, this seeming quest for history becomes an interpretive task in itself. Commentators who want to see the parable as subversive (the seed becomes a tree, and this is contrary to nature) favor Luke's version—and its tree—and claim that Mark missed the point by changing the image to a shrub. Yet it is just as possible that Jesus changed his wording along the way, as any good storyteller would. Good storytellers vary the details of their tales, depending on their audiences and their moods. "Viewing Jesus as some sort of automaton who had to make each of his pronouncements the same yesterday, today, and forever robs him of his humanity and his narrative genius," Levine observes.

So Jesus told a story about a mustard seed, some kind of sprouting, and a growth that can shelter birds. Was it mustard? Was it a tree or a shrub? Were the birds simply birds or meant to represent the nations of the world? These questions remain open.

Before we can start to interpret the parable as Jesus's audience would have heard it, we need to weed out a few incorrect interpretations. The major faulty approaches see the parable of the mustard seed as having to do with Jewish purity laws. A number of commentators like to see Jesus with this parable as challenging the purity laws and all of Jewish identity in the process. Such commentators, who usually have no experience with keeping kosher or honoring the Sabbath or otherwise living a traditional Jewish life, tend to see purity as a problem rather than as a blessing. This, says Levine, is a major misreading of Jesus.

How do commentators come to see the parable of the Mustard Seed as being about purity laws? First, many interpreters bring in this concern for purity laws by reading the parable of the Mustard Seed in light of the parable of the Leaven:

> And again he said, "To what should I compare the kingdom of God? It is like yeast that a woman took and mixed in with three measures of flour until all of it was leavened."
>
> *Luke 13:20-21*

*He told them another parable: "The kingdom of heaven is like yeast that a woman took and mixed in with three measures of flour until all of it was leavened."*

Matthew 13:33

These interpreters also see the parable of the Leaven as being about uncleanness and impurity. However, the parable of the Leaven is not about impurity either. Just as there is nothing impure about a mustard seed or mustard, so there is nothing impure about leaven or baked bread.

If we want to read these two parables together, then we need to develop another interpretation. They both have something growing from small to large, they both have the theme of secrecy (the yeast is "hidden"—that is the verb that actually appears in the Greek text—while the seed grows out of sight), and they both point out that one small action can have an effect on a large number of people (or birds).

Second, interpreters who see the parable of the Mustard Seed as being about purity cite biblical prohibitions against mixing diverse kinds, like mustard seeds "tossed" into the garden, therefore polluting it. Then the mustard seed is taken to be a weed. "Thus is it uncultivated," writes Levine, "in violation of purity laws, out of place, deviant, and so on."

Such interpretations can't take root, however. There is no problem with different vegetables or herbs in the same garden. There's nothing transgressive or impure about the mustard seed in the garden. Nor does Jesus mention any other plants, so there's no reason to believe that there's a problem with mixing crops in this case. Moreover, mustard has numerous uses, from spicing food to providing medicinal qualities.

The parable of the Mustard Seed and the parable of the Leaven can be read together by simply observing that in going from yeast to bread, and from seed to plant, something desirable emerges. We can't do a lot with yeast and a seed, but for both, the potential for something great is present.

Now that we've established some productive and not-so-productive ways to interpret the mustard seed and its tree, we turn to the birds. There are nearly fifty mentions of "birds of the air" in the Old Testament. For birds in trees, we can look to the Psalms, where birds build their nests in the cedars of Lebanon (Psalm 104:16-17). These are positive associations, but interpreters tend to focus on images of birds in trees that symbolize fallen empires (Ezekiel 31 and Daniel 4). Then it's the strong mustard plant (and not the cedar) that represents the kingdom of heaven.

Would any of these interpretations have occurred to first-century Galileans? Birds in a tree was not exactly a common image for empire. "Birds of the air" is common in the Bible, but when a Jewish storyteller speaks about the birds of the air, a first-century audience is not going to think, "He's talking about Gentiles." When Jesus talks about birds elsewhere, he's just talking about birds. Levine writes, "Sometimes a seed is just a seed, a bird is just a bird, and a tree is just a tree."

The parable doesn't have to be about empire, or international relations, and it certainly is not about purity. There is nothing problematic about mustard. But the parable does say something about the contrast between small and large. And it does speak to seeds and birds, growth and shelter. Since these are the main parts of the parable, this is probably where we can derive several more healthy, and tasty, interpretations.

If we say that the parable says that great things come from small things, we don't get much of a challenge. Instead, we should think about exactly what great things arise. Perhaps the plant is a gift of nature, offering something that many (people or birds) can appreciate. The plant is something small that, when allowed to grow, has great effects. And the birds of the air make nests in the mustard plant and make for themselves a way to survive. Humanity and nature work together, and all creation benefits.

We also learn that some things need to be left alone. If we continue to bother the dough, it will not rise. If we continue to bother the seed, it will not germinate. We don't have to pay attention, all the time, to everything. Often we just need to get out of the way. The woman puts the yeast in the dough. The man plants or tosses the seed. What arises is focused not on the person doing the original action, but on the results.

Or perhaps we should think about that giant tree—for most mustard seeds produce only small bushes. Can we imagine extraordinary growth from ordinary things: are we open to surprise or mystery?

Or again, perhaps we might be that seed—seeming to be so small now, but having the potential to be great, or to do great things. That is a particularly good message for little children. Those great things may well come, but we also need to be patient.

Finally, can we imagine that the kingdom of heaven is present, in potential, in our own ovens or our own gardens? All it takes is someone willing to plant the seed, to take the first step. It will grow in the dark, warm earth. All that is needed is for someone to hide yeast in dough, and that will rise in the warm, dark oven. When we taste that bit of mustard or that bite of bread, we can imagine the kingdom all around us, even inside of us.

When we see the birds nesting in branches, can we imagine the kingdom present? Are they part of the kingdom too? Will we notice if the birds are gone?

The kingdom comes when humanity and nature work together, as we provide for others and provide for ourselves.

---

When we see the birds nesting in branches, can we imagine the kingdom present? Are they part of the kingdom too? Will we notice if the birds are gone?

---

## QUESTIONS FOR REFLECTION

1. The parable of the Mustard Seed appears in three Gospels. What are the differences among the accounts? What do you make of those differences?
2. These elements of the parable are the same in all three versions: a small mustard seed, branches, and birds taking shelter. When you have heard this parable, how have you interpreted those elements?
3. Levine writes, "There is no challenge in hearing that from small beginnings come great things." If that message is not the parable's provocation, what is? What interpretations of this parable have you heard or been taught?
4. A number of parables begin with, "The kingdom of God is like..." How do you understand the term "the kingdom of God"? Is it a place? A time? A new form of social relationships? Explain your response.

5. Some interpreters see the mustard seed as impure and therefore a violation of Jewish purity laws. Why would a mustard seed be impure? How does Levine explain and discount this interpretation?

6. Levine brings this parable into conversation with the parable of the Leaven:

> He told them another parable: "The kingdom of heaven is like yeast that a woman took and mixed in with three measures of flour until all of it was leavened."
>
> Matthew 13:33

What are the similarities between the yeast and the mustard seed? What do you think is the message of this parable? What does it say about the kingdom of heaven?

7. Both the parable of the Mustard Seed and the parable of the Leaven take place in the domestic world. What does this say about the kingdom of God? About our homes and gardens? About the things we make and sow?

8. Where do you see the idea of potential in each of these parables? What might Jesus be saying with these images of potential?

9. The mustard seed is not the smallest seed, but it is tiny compared to the tree it produces. What does this symbolism suggest to you? What might it mean that birds come to nest in this comparatively large tree?

10. Putting aside symbolism and allegory, Levine writes, "Sometimes a seed is just a seed, a bird is just a bird, and a tree is just a tree." With that in mind, what could Jesus have meant by telling this story?

## PERSONAL RESPONSE

Read the following excerpts from *Short Stories by Jesus*. Consider the questions that follow in the context of the parable discussed in this chapter and your own personal experience.

Like the vast amount of bread the woman baked, the mustard plant offers more than a single person can use. The invitation to partake is a universal one, as the birds so neatly demonstrate. Instead of looking at the plant as a noxious weed, we might be better off seeing it as part of the gifts of nature; something so small, allowed to do what it naturally does, produces prodigious effects.

- How does this explanation change your interpretation of the parable of the Mustard Seed?
- What things in your life bring joy and goodness when they are allowed to flourish?

Sometimes we need to *get out of the way*. We are not always the focus; sometimes we are the facilitator for something bigger than ourselves. The woman hides the yeast in the dough; whether people knew she did the baking or not remains unstated. The man plants, or even tosses, the seed. Who sowed it is much less important than the tree into which the seed grows. The final image is not a focus on the human actor, but on the results of the action.

- What projects have you been involved in that required you to back away?

- Is it hard for you to get something started and then leave it alone?
- What does this interpretation of the parable say about the kingdom of God?

The challenge of the parable can be much homier: don't ask "when" the kingdom comes or "where" it is. The when is in its own good time—as long as it takes for seed to sprout and dough to rise. The where is that it is already present, inchoate, in the world. The kingdom is present when humanity and nature work together, and we do what we were put here to do—to go out on a limb to provide for others, and ourselves as well.

- What does it mean to you to envision the kingdom as already happening in your home and in the world?
- Before you read this chapter, did you see the mustard seed and the yeast as symbols of providing for others?
- What message do you think Jesus was trying to communicate to his original audience?
- What message do you receive?

## Session 5

# The Laborers in the Vineyard

### THE PARABLE

*"For the kingdom of heaven is like a landowner who went out early in the morning to hire laborers for his vineyard. After agreeing with the laborers for the usual daily wage, he sent them into his vineyard. When he went out about nine o'clock, he saw others standing idle in the marketplace; and he said to them, 'You also go into the vineyard, and I will pay you whatever is right.' So they went. When he went out again about noon and about three o'clock, he did the same. And about five o'clock he went out and found others standing around; and he said to them, 'Why are you standing here idle all day?' They said to him, 'Because no one has hired us.' He said to them, 'You also go into the vineyard.' When evening came, the owner of the vineyard said to his manager, 'Call the laborers and give them their pay, beginning*

*with the last and then going to the first.' When those hired about five o'clock came, each of them received the usual daily wage. Now when the first came, they thought they would receive more; but each of them also received the usual daily wage. And when they received it, they grumbled against the landowner, saying, 'These last worked only one hour, and you have made them equal to us who have borne the burden of the day and the scorching heat.' But he replied to one of them, 'Friend, I am doing you no wrong; did you not agree with me for the usual daily wage? Take what belongs to you and go; I choose to give to this last the same as I give to you. Am I not allowed to do what I choose with what belongs to me? Or are you envious because I am generous?' So the last will be first, and the first will be last."*

*Matthew 20:1-16*

## CHAPTER SUMMARY

The parable tells the story of a landowner who went out early to hire workers for his vineyard. He gets together a group of workers and agrees with them that he will pay them each a denarius, the usual daily wage, for work through the day. Then he keeps going out throughout the day, continuing to hire workers at various hours. When quitting time arrives, he asks his manager to pay the workers, starting with the last hired. They each get the expected denarius. So do all the others. The first hired are upset: they do not think it is fair that they, who have worked all day long, should get the same wage as the last hired who had only done an hour or so of work. They complain. The "lord of the vineyard" (Matthew 20:8; the NRSV translates "the owner of the vineyard") defends his right to pay as he sees fit, and he sends them away. The parable ends with the saying, "So the last will be first, and the first will be last" (Matthew 20:16).

The usual title of this parable suggests some immediate interpretation. "The Laborers in the Vineyard" puts the focus first on the laborers, or "workers" as they are sometimes called, and second on the location, the vineyard. With this title, the reader is prompted to identify with the laborers and not the landowner. Moreover, most readers identify the landowner with God. Reading the Greek expression in Matthew 20:8 literally as "the lord of the vineyard" enhances this allegorical association. Then, because the prophet Isaiah presents the "Song of the Vineyard" (Isaiah 5:1-7) in which the Vineyard represents Israel, readers see the vineyard in our parable as having something to do with the people Israel (the Jewish people), the land of Israel, or both. Putting the focus on the vineyard prompts the jump to allegory since the vineyard is already understood in Jewish culture to be God's property. Once we are on God's property, the parable according to many interpreters must be about salvation.

Over the years interpreters have generally seen the householder as God. That's not an impossible reading. The problems come in, however, when we start imposing allegorical readings on the various people in the labor pool. Often, interpreters cast the first hired—those grumbling and seeking to be compensated for their work—as Pharisees, who are similarly grumbling and resistant to Jesus and Jesus's ministry. Or those first hired are identified as the Jews, who look at obedience to Torah as a form of difficult if not impossible labor. Still other interpreters see the first hired as Jews who rejected the inclusion of Gentiles in the church, and the last hired as the impure or Gentiles. Such interpretations are, simply, wrong. As Amy-Jill Levine advises, "When Jewish practice or Jewish society becomes the negative foil to Jesus or the church, we do well to reread the parable."

All the workers in the parable are part of the same labor pool. The parable has nothing to do with Jewish-Gentile relations, purity laws, or the difficulty of following Torah. Those who read this symbolism as well as seeing the various workers as different groups of people might also tend toward anti-Jewish readings, such as seeing the burden of the Jewish law in the workers "who have borne the burden of the day and the scorching heat" (Matthew 20:12).

Such readings only serve to separate Jesus from his own Jewish context. Just as unfortunate, they ignore the concrete economic and employment cases the parable is making. The parable has a very real context—the world of employment, the difficult lives of day laborers, and the responsibility of those with resources to make sure that everyone has enough to live on. Levine suggests alternate titles: "the parable of the Complaining Day Laborers," or "the parable of the Surprising Salaries."

As Levine points out, Jesus was more interested in talking about how to love one's neighbor than in describing the theology one needs in order to get into heaven. What if we look at this parable and see real workers and real landowners who hire them? Jesus wanted to think about questions of whether people have enough to eat or shelter for the night. This parable might help answer real-life questions like this.

Still other interpreters, agreeing that the parable does address economic issues, see the landowner as exploitative. By paying the last hired the same wage as those who had been working since early in the morning, the landowner, in this configuration, sets the workers against one another and thus makes it more difficult for them to come together and unionize. Such readings, while speaking to today's labor issues, do not fit the parable. Jesus made it clear that the first-hired agreed to the usually daily wage, the "denarius of the day" (Levine's translation). The landowner does not show himself to be exploitative. Yet we still need to address why he pays the workers as he does.

Levine suggests a simpler option: "What if we saw the parable...as dealing with labor relations...? What if we saw [the parable] as about what God would have us do not to earn salvation, but to love our neighbor?"

The landowner in Greek is an *oikodespotes*. In the translation above, the NRSV has "landowner," but a better understanding of this word would be householder. It is possible that he represents God in this parable and that the vineyard represents Israel (the land and/or the people), but so far he is just an employer in search of workers to harvest his vineyard. He is not able to offer less than the "usual daily wage"; he "agrees with" the workers to pay this much for their work. They have a contractual arrangement. There is nothing unusual about the story so far.

Things start to get a little strange when 9 a.m. rolls around and the householder goes out again. He finds more workers "standing idle in the marketplace," as the NRSV reads (Matthew 20:3). However, Levine notes that the Greek word used to describe the workers here, *agroi*, means literally "without work." This is something different from standing around doing nothing. Perhaps they are waiting for someone else to hire them. Harvest time means that all the local vineyards would be in need of people to work the fields. The householder hires them without making any formal agreement; he says he will pay them a just wage. Should we think he is up to something shady? Today, employers might take advantage of unemployed (and undocumented) workers. But we can probably take this householder at his word. Were he to cheat the workers, he would not be able to get anyone else to harvest his fields. Based on the parable so far, we have no reason not to trust the householder, even if it is odd that he did not, the first time, hire the full complement of workers he needed.

But then things become downright weird. The householder heads out three more times, well into the evening, and hires more workers. Levine observes, "That our householder returns to the market over and over again suggests either that he is clueless about the number of workers he needs, that he has an insufficient number of workers although he has hired everyone available, or that he has another agenda." It's starting to look like this householder might have another agenda after all. He continues to hire people, but the parable doesn't say that he needs the extra labor.

The parable also doesn't explain why all these unemployed workers are in the marketplace. Some surmise that the last ones hired were old and infirm, but the parable says nothing to support this idea. We don't know why workers were there at the end of the workday, still looking for work. Others say that the last hired workers represent the Gentile nations, who came comparatively late to the worship of the God of Israel, but again, the parable offers nothing in support of this allegorical reading. In fact, the parable cites no difference among the first hired workers and those hired at 3 p.m. or 5 p.m. Allegorical interpretations fail. Nor are they needed. Since time immemorial, people have looked for work and not been able to find it. There is nothing surprising about people lining up to get work, and not finding it. There is, however, something tragic about such a situation.

In the next part of the parable, the language shifts. Jesus refers to the householder as "the lord of the vineyard" (20:8; the NRSV translates this as "the owner of the vineyard," which loses the divine reference inherent in the Greek). It is possible to read the householder as God. It is equally possible to see him as the one who controls the vineyard, since the Greek term *kyrios* can mean "lord" or "master." Is the landowner God, or is he one in the position of ruler since he has all the resources that others need?

At the end of the parable, the householder/lord has the last word. "Friend, I am doing you no wrong," he addresses the grumbling workers. By calling them "friend," it is clear that he is upset with them. "Friend" as a form of address appears only three times in Matthew: here, in this parable; in the parable of the Wedding Banquet where the king asks, "Friend, how did you get in here without a wedding robe?" and then tosses him out (22:12); and when Jesus says to Judas, "Friend, do what you are here to do" (26:50). The appearance of this word connects the irritated laborers with betrayal and punishment.

The householder has a point in these last lines. He hasn't done anything wrong, or treated anyone unfairly. He paid the first workers what he promised them, a denarius. Similarly, he paid the other workers what he thought was "right," as he'd promised them. The householder has treated the workers equally, but the first-hired workers are upset and resentful.

Perhaps it is these workers who are in the wrong in this story; they don't want those hired last to have a living wage. Worse, all of these workers were part of the same initial labor pool. They were all likely present at 6 a.m., waiting for work. They all knew what it was like not to be hired, not to have enough money to feed their families. Each time the landowner hired another group, that group happily accepted the invitation. They forgot how worried they had been about not having a job, and they forgot the people left in the marketplace. They showed no care for their fellow workers.

The parable proper ends with the landowner's comment, "Or are you envious because I am generous?" The saying, "So the last will be first, and the first will be last," which appears elsewhere in the Gospels, actually contradicts what the parable is saying. Everyone is paid the same amount; as the first-hired complain, they have all been made equal. We might also wonder if we want the last to be first and the first to be last. Would we be better if we were all side by side?

Levine agrees with interpreters who propose that the workers should have been happy for one another since now everyone has received a decent wage and can provide for their families. "Indeed, they should have been," she writes, "and with this note we may be getting to the provocation of the parable."

This parable contains a provocative message for then and for today. The message is simple, practical, and economic. The house-holder fulfills his agreement with the first hired, and then he pay a "just" wage to the others. He uses his resources as he sees fit, and in doing so, he makes sure that everyone has a job.

Although the first-hired complain, their complaints will get no traction. All they could finally say is that the landowner was generous. He hired everyone. He paid everyone a fair wage.

The parable suggests that householders, if they have the resources, should provide opportunities for people in search of work. If the householder can afford it, he should continue to employ everyone he can and pay them a fair wage. Paying workers (regardless of the amount of work) allows him to provide for them while allowing the workers to work, and thus retain their dignity. This is what the householder *should* be doing; this is what he does.

Jesus, who did state that "it is easier for a camel to go through the eye of a needle than for someone who is rich to enter the kingdom of God" (Matthew 19:24, only a few verses before our parable), often focuses on the responsibility of the rich. Here, the rich man provides the daily denarius, the living wage, the fair wage, to all the workers. Jesus is also concerned about how we love our neighbors as ourselves. Here, in the voice of the "lord of the vineyard," he condemns the first-hired for not advocating for their fellow workers, for complaining that these fellow workers received the same amount as they did.

---

**Here, the rich man provides the daily denarius, the living wage, the fair wage, to all the workers. Jesus is also concerned about how we love our neighbors as ourselves. Here, in the voice of the "lord of the vineyard," he condemns the first-hired for not advocating for their fellow workers, for complaining that these fellow workers received the same amount as they did.**

---

Perhaps the next day, those first-hired will be left behind as others get the jobs in the vineyard. Will they complain about a generous landowner then? And what of those last-hired: will they who feared not having any money at the end of the day advocate for those left behind? Will we?

In the end, everyone has enough. "The pressing reality," writes Levine, is "that people need jobs and that others have excess funds.... And in that story, we learn what it means to act as God acts, with generosity to all." We also learn about our responsibilities to others, and that may be the harder lesson.

# Questions for Reflection

1. When you first read this parable, what was your image of laborers in the vineyard? What did they look like? What were they doing? Did you identify with them? Why or why not?

2. Similarly, what was your image of the householder? Levine points out that the word *oikodespotes* can be translated as "landowner," or, more accurately in her view, "householder." What are your impressions of those two terms? Does one or the other change your view of this person? Do you identify with him?

3. Levine proposes alternate titles for the parable: "The Conscientious Boss," "Debating a Fair Wage," "Lessons for Both Management and Employees." How does focusing the parable on the contemporary reality of employment rather than the ancient context of laboring in a vineyard change how you understand its message?

4. If you worked in an office and the worker in the next cubicle over was paid the same salary for fewer hours of the same work, how would you feel? Would you speak to your boss about it? Why or why not?

5. What anti-Jewish readings spring up around this parable? What unfortunate interpretations come from allegorizing the first-hired laborers as Jews?

6. How do you interpret the last line of the parable, "So the last will be first, and the first will be last" (Matthew 20:16)? Do you think it was an original part of the parable? Do you want anyone to be last? If so, whom and why?

7. The householder goes back into the marketplace in search of workers again and again throughout the day. Why do you think he does that?

8. Do you think the disgruntled first-hired laborers were wrong to complain? Should they have been happy for the last-hired laborers to receive a decent wage? Explain your response.

9. Levine posits that the householder acts as God acts, and therefore serves as a model or reflection of the divine. Do you see the householder as a reflection of God? Why or why not?

10. Do you agree with Levine's estimation that this parable is more about love of neighbor than about salvation? Why or why not? Which is more challenging, that the parable is about taking care of each other, or ways to get into heaven?

## PERSONAL RESPONSE

Read the following excerpts from *Short Stories by Jesus*. Consider the questions that follow in the context of the parable discussed in this chapter and your own personal experience.

> To those who ask today, "Are you saved?" Jesus might well respond, "The better question is, 'Do your children have enough to eat?' or 'Do you have shelter for the night?'" This parable helps us ask those more pressing, more visceral questions.

- How does the parable help you ask those questions?
- What kinds of answers does it suggest?

- Before you read this chapter, did you consider this parable to have a message about care for family or social justice?

What if we saw the parable not as about exploitative landowners and workers facing extreme poverty, but as dealing with labor relations in a relatively prosperous period? What if we saw it as about what God would have us do not to earn salvation, but to love our neighbor?

- What opportunities for neighbor love do you see in this parable?
- Have you ever been in a situation like this, either as a worker or a supervisor?
- What message comes through in this parable when we see it as simply a story about people rather than create symbols out of the characters?

This householder is no evil tyrant or elitist exploiter. It is the laborers—who do not want the last hired to have a living wage—who are in the wrong.

- Do you agree with this statement? Why or why not?
- What do you think of the householder's treatment of the workers?
- Would you do the same thing?
- Would you be angry if you were one of the first-hired workers?
- How would you feel if you were one of the last-hired workers?

## Session 6

# The Widow and the Judge

### THE PARABLE

*Then Jesus told them a parable about their need to pray always and not to lose heart. He said, "In a certain city there was a judge who neither feared God nor had respect for people. In that city there was a widow who kept coming to him and saying, 'Grant me justice against my opponent.' For a while he refused; but later he said to himself, 'Though I have no fear of God and no respect for anyone, yet because this widow keeps bothering me, I will grant her justice, so that she may not wear me out by continually coming.'" And the Lord said, "Listen to what the unjust judge says. And will not God grant justice to his chosen ones who cry to him day and night? Will he delay long in helping them? I tell you, he will quickly grant justice to them. And yet, when the Son of Man comes, will he find faith on earth?"*

*Luke 18:1-8*

## CHAPTER SUMMARY

Jewish tradition mandates that God has particular concern for the poor, the widow, the orphan, and the stranger, and therefore so should we (see, for example, Exodus 22:22; Deuteronomy 10:18; 14:29; and elsewhere). From this notice of society's more vulnerable members comes the stereotype of the poor, helpless, victimized widow. But the Bible also consistently shatters that stereotype.

Tamar, Naomi, Ruth, Orpah, Abigail, Judith—all of these are biblical widows who act with intelligence, agency, and bravery. According to the stereotype, we expect widows to be weak, but these women demonstrate remarkable strength. We expect widows to be the victims, but the opposite happens in the stories told of these women. We expect widows to be helpless, but instead Tamar, Ruth, and their sisters wind up helping both themselves and others. These women defy the stereotype of the poor, helpless, victimized widow, so much so that we might begin to question the stereotype itself. Equally unconventional is the so-called importuning widow in this parable. She "similarly shatters the stereotype, even as she epitomizes the strength, cleverness, and very problematic motives of many of her predecessors."

But that stereotype remains strong. The widow in our parable has been domesticated by years of interpretation, starting with Luke the Evangelist. Amy-Jill Levine notes that there is a great deal of controversy about how much of the parable came from Jesus, and how much was edited or composed by Luke. Most people agree that 18:2-5 is the core of the parable and comes from Jesus. Levine posits, "Jesus told a very short story about a judge and a widow, both with problematic characteristics; the judge is not inclined to grant the widow's request, but because of her persistence and her threats, he does. That's it." Our interpretive task begins and ends with these four verses. What might the original audience have thought of this very short story?

Luke assigns a message to her story straightaway: "Then Jesus told them a parable about their need to pray always and not to lose heart" (18:1). Instead of presenting her as an independent woman who relentlessly goes after the judge until she gets what she wants, this verse sees our widow less as a public agitator and more as a model of quiet prayer. Luke confirms this impression by closing the parable with the question: "And will not God grant justice to his chosen ones who cry to him day and night?" (18:7).

Luke gives us a picture of a widow—we can import all those stereotypes of the widow as poor, elderly, frail, helpless—crying out to God day and night. Here she joins the stereotype of other meek, mild, dependent, and powerless widows. Luke has a penchant for such images. Luke tells us about Anna, the eighty-four-year-old widow who never left the Temple (Luke 2:36-38). Yet whereas Luke notes that she "began...to speak about the child [Jesus] to all who were looking for the redemption of Jerusalem," we never hear her words. The elderly man with whom she is paired, Simeon, does all the talking. Luke mentions the "many widows in Israel" who suffered under "a severe famine" (Luke 4:25), as well as the widow of Zarephath (4:26). But in this recounting, it is Elijah who helps the widow; her own story, bravery, and agency are ignored. Luke mentions the widow of Nain, whose son Jesus raises from the dead (Luke 7:11-15). We have widows who are exploited by rapacious scribes (Luke 20:47) and the poor widow who puts her last two coins into the Temple treasury (Luke 21:2-4). There are the Hellenist widows overlooked during the daily distribution (Acts 6:1), and the widows who mourn the death of Tabitha (Acts 9:39-41). Across the Gospel of Luke, widows are figures of piety, pity, or both. Conceiving of the widow of our parable along similar lines fits the pattern.

However, the parables of Jesus give women power. Jesus speaks of a woman (could she be a widow?) who loses her coin, finds it, and then throws a celebration for all of her women friends. A woman hides yeast in dough, and so through her baking gives rise (as it were) to the kingdom of heaven. Matthew (25:1-12) gives us the parable of the wise and foolish virgins (the NRSV reads "bridesmaids") who travel by themselves, have funds to purchase oil for their lamps, and wait for an overdue groom. All these women are active, independent, and use their own resources.

The widow in our parable is better compared to the women in Jesus's other parables than to the widows in Luke. The widow in our parable confronts the judge and doesn't give up until he is persuaded. Jesus himself interacted with women who were doing things other than praying and fasting: Mary (his mother), the sisters Martha and Mary, the Samaritan woman at the well, the Syrophoenician woman, the woman with the hemorrhage, Peter's mother-in-law, Mary Magdalene, and so on. These are all active women, who seek what they want, who appear in public, who have access to resources, and who stand out for their courage and convictions. There is no reason to stereotype them, or to box them into ancillary roles.

And there is no reason to stereotype widows, whether in the Bible or today. Widows, though, don't conform to stereotypes. They, "like all women, like all humans, have complex personalities and not always transparent motives," writes Levine. She also observes, "Telling a widow in a church today that she is helpless, oppressed, or needy may not be good news. It may also not be accurate."

As with the other parables, the title we give this story of the widow and the judge makes a difference. Traditionally, our text is known as the "parable of the Importuning Widow." To importune is to ask someone repeatedly and persistently for something, and it has a sense of begging. Therefore, in this version the widow is set up as someone weak from the very title. Titles like the parable of the Persistent Widow, the Tenacious Widow, or the Nagging Widow might not be flattering, but at least they give the widow some strength and agency. Here we opt simply for the parable of the Widow and the Judge. Based on cultural stereotypes, we are likely to see the widow as helpless and vulnerable, and so we identify with her and support her case. We conclude that this widow must be a decent person. However, the parable is more challenging than that. According to the NRSV's translation, the widow continually asks the judge to grant her "justice" against her opponent. Levine points out that the Greek word used here is not the one usually translated as justice (which would be *dikaiosyne*). Instead, the word she uses is *ekdikeo*, which has more the sense of "let me be avenged." Thus the word translated "justice" really means "vengeance." It is the same term that appears in the phrase, "Vengeance is mine, I will repay, says the Lord" (Romans 12:19). Is the widow asking for "justice," or is she asking for "vengeance"? Do we even know the difference between the two? Since this case lacks details (does she want money from someone? someone to be thrown in jail?), we have no way of knowing what kind of request she is making. Considering biblical precedents about vengeance, we can assume that the widow isn't interested in reaching an agreement with her adversary, but seeks to punish him.

Moreover, Jesus advises in the Sermon on the Mount, "Come to terms quickly with your accuser while you are on the way to court with him" (Matthew 5:25). The widow has not done this. Indeed, we never meet her opponent. Do we automatically judge him as in the wrong, because we want to believe that the widow is righteous? Might there be two sides to this story, and have we rushed to judgment?

We also want to side with the widow because we don't like this judge, whom Jesus describes as not fearing God and not caring about what people think. The parable is sometimes called the "parable of the Unjust Judge." Yet that "Unjust Judge" title doesn't have a basis in the parable itself. The only time he is called "unjust" is in the comments after the parable, "The Lord said, 'Listen to what the unjust judge says'" (18:6). At what point does the judge then become unjust? Was he always so, or does he become unjust in granting the widow what she wants, not because her case is valid, but because he fears that she will punch him in the face?

Indeed, what are we to make of this judge? Most of what the parable says comes by way of his interior thoughts. Is he the protagonist of this parable? Are we supposed to identify with him, or with the widow? Or with neither?

The truth is that we know very little about the widow in this parable. It is true that some widows are poor and vulnerable, just like some laborers are exploited. Levine wants to challenge stereotypes here. Not all widows are meek, helpless, and without agency. Think about widows you know. How many of them fit the stereotype above?

When we do historical work, we find that women in first-century Jewish society owned their own homes, had access to their own funds, had freedom of travel, attended the synagogue and the Temple, and could plead their own cases in courts. The system was by no means egalitarian (neither is twenty-first-century America), but it was not dreadful for women either. Some widows suffered and had a hard time, but it was by no means the norm. And so we realize how little we know about our widow: was she rich or poor? Young or old? In the right, or in the wrong?

The parable tells us that the widow is located in a city. Would a person in a metropolitan environment regard her differently than a person from rural Galilee? Does she have big-city sophistication, or is she among the urban poor? We know she is persistent—it's not cheap or easy to "keep coming" to the court (18:3). "The widow might well be destitute, oppressed, and desperate," writes Levine. "She may also be wealthy, powerful, and vengeful. Or she may be somewhere in between." Readers must resist the urge to stereotype her in order to hear the challenge of the parable.

The judge presents his own mysteries. According to Luke, the judge is "unjust" (18:6). In the larger frame, he is a negative version of God. But as for the parable itself, we only know that the judge "neither feared God nor had respect for people" (18:2). Later in the parable, the judge uses the same words to describe himself: "I have no fear of God and no respect for anyone" (18:4). What we see is what we get. The judge does not fear God, but this is not the same as being unjust. Being stupid is not necessarily the same thing as being sinful (a point seen also with the prodigal son). Jesus himself seems to have a dislike for judges and does not want to judge or be a judge. In Luke 6:37, he says, "Do not judge, and you will not be judged; do not condemn, and you will not be condemned. Forgive, and you will be forgiven." Curiously, neither the judge nor the widow is predisposed to do either. There is no forgiving in this courtroom, but there is judging, of a sort. So the judge does not fear God or respect people, and the widow at the very least does not respect this judge, considering the persistence with which she continues to approach him even as he is just as persistent with refusing her. Plus, she may be demanding vengeance. They are a good match for each other.

The last line of the parable offers the judge's decision: "Because this widow keeps bothering me, I will grant her justice, so that she may not wear me out by continually coming" (18:5). Looking closely at the original Greek gives some insight into what is going on here. "Wear me out" is a boxing term, and a better translation might be "strike me in the face" or "give me a black eye." The judge appears to be scared of a physical blow, and this—not justice— is what pushes him into a decision. Further, "grant her justice" literally means "avenge her." The judge facilitates this vengeance. "The parable proper ends with the judge's decision," Levine writes, "and so it ends as a story about corruption, violence, and vengefulness."

Luke domesticates this parable by providing an opening and closing frame. Luke presents this parable as being about the "need to pray always and not to lose heart" (18:1). This interpretation is an allegory, and there is no reason to think that Jesus's original audience would have heard this story and thought that it had anything to do with prayer.

This parable—taken without Luke's explanation—is difficult to understand. The parable challenges us by challenging stereotypes. Widows, usually seen as weak and powerless, may in fact be powerful and vengeful. We want to think of widows as needing to be protected, and also nonviolent. But the widow in our parable is certainly not a woman who "loves her enemies" (Luke 6:27). Nor is our judge a model of loving others.

The parable challenges us by keeping us from having a positive identification with either character. Neither is particularly likeable, and this is uncomfortable.

The parable is also uncomfortable because of its lack of closure. All we get here is a joint plan for the widow and the judge to take vengeance on some unnamed adversary. There is no attempt to find reconciliation.

The widow gets her way by threatening the judge with violence. But is violence ever justified? If so, under what circumstances? Do we support the widow when she threatens violence, because we picture her as old and frail? Would we support the same threat but coming from a muscular man of nineteen? Do we support the widow because we regard the judge as unjust? If so, are we also supporting an unjust system?

As for the judge, he acts to protect himself. What, then, is the value of justice in his court? In agreeing to give the widow what she wants, has he done the right thing for the wrong reasons—he gives her what she wants, but only because he fears what she will do to him? Or has he done the wrong thing for the right reason—he issues an unjust judgment (remember, we do not have the details of her case, and she may be asking for vengeance rather than justice) because he does not want to suffer bodily harm?

---

Jesus demands that we actually think about the difference between justice and vengeance, that we challenge our stereotypes of widows and judges, that we refuse to rush to judgment because we don't have all the information needed to make a fair decision, that we don't judge.

---

We may dismiss the parable entirely, opting instead for a more compassionate approach than what these two characters have to offer. That is what Luke does. But Jesus demands more from us. Jesus demands that we actually think about the difference between justice and vengeance, that we challenge our stereotypes of widows and judges, that we refuse to rush to judgment because we don't have all the information needed to make a fair decision, that we don't judge.

In the parable of the Widow and the Judge, vengeance rules. The widow's desire for vengeance overshadows any desire for justice. In her work with prisoners at Nashville's maximum-security prison, Levine encounters many who see themselves as victims of vengeance, for example, people who have been in prison for over forty years, who have the support of prison psychiatrists but who are refused parole by the parole board. Were we the victims of violent crime, or serving on a parole board, we might very well find ourselves on the side of vengeance. At what point does a prison sentence become vengeance rather than justice?

The parable forces us to examine our own stereotypes, not only of widows and judges, but of the entire justice system and its fairness. "Jesus was invested in fairness, reconciliation, and compassion," writes Levine, but this parable doesn't demonstrate any fairness. The judge's decision is not based on the justice of God; it is based on being threatened. By telling this story, Jesus compels us to consider our own moral compass, and that of whatever system administers justice. Where, asks Jesus, is justice to be found?

## QUESTIONS FOR REFLECTION

1. Before you read this chapter, what was your impression of widows? Are you a widow? Do you know any widows personally? Any in the media? What stereotypes exist about widows?
2. How do widows in the Bible defy common stereotypes? How does the widow in this parable do so?
3. How has the widow in this parable been "domesticated"?
4. Luke suggests that the parable is about the need for constant prayer. Do you think that interpretation works? What are some problems with this story as an example of prayer?
5. Levine offers alternate titles for the parable: "Persistent Widow," "Tenacious Widow," and "Nagging Widow."

How do these titles affect your interpretation of the parable, or your impression of the widow?

6. In the NRSV, the widow seeks "justice against my opponent" (Luke 18:3). Levine suggests that a better translation might say that the widow wants to be "avenged." What is the difference between these? Explain your answer.

7. Do you have any preconceived notions about judges? If so, what are they?

8. Why do you think the judge finally gives in to the widow?

9. Does this parable contain a message about reconciliation? If so, what is it?

10. Are there any situations in which it is appropriate to persist in questioning, or to threaten violence?

11. Whom do you support in this parable? Does anyone come out looking positive?

12. What does the parable suggest about both justice and judging?

## PERSONAL RESPONSE

Read the following excerpts from *Short Stories by Jesus.* Consider the questions that follow in the context of the parable discussed in this chapter and your own personal experience.

> Parables are designed to shake up one's worldview, to question the conventional. If a manager can be dishonest, a tax collector righteous, a landowner generous enough to provide a living wage to everyone in the marketplace, and a judge neither God-fearing nor respectful toward the people, surely a widow can be vengeful.

- What is your opinion of the widow and the judge in this parable?
- Levine challenges us to abandon stereotypes. How does doing so affect your interpretation of the parable?

The Greek uses a boxing term: the judge is concerned that the widow will give him a black eye. Whether we take this expression literally and see the woman as threatening violence or metaphorically and see the woman as suggesting humiliation or mortification will impact how we assess her character.

- Before you read this chapter, did you see the widow as making a violent threat against the judge?
- How does that change what you think of her character?
- Is there any situation in your own life that would push you to threaten violence against another person?

The parable proper ends with the judge's decision and so it ends as a story about corruption, violence, and vengefulness. Stereotypes of judges and widows both fall. Justice is not clearly rendered. Has the widow made the judge "just" by convincing him to rule in her favor, or has she corrupted him? What would the widow's opponent think? What do we think?

- Consider Levine's questions above. How does this situation look from the point of view of the widow's adversary?
- Is there anyone in this parable that you identify with?

Printed in the USA

CPSIA information can be obtained
at www.ICGtesting.com
Printed in the USA
FSHW021521150219
55701FS